"What could be more counterc[u]ltural[?] A
church that chooses generosity [and gives away]
money year after year? In the mecca of materialism lies an
oasis of liberality—a place where Christ followers are modeling revolutionary giving in a culture consumed with getting.
And yet, as they have blessed others, God has kept his promises to bless them. The root of the word *miserable* is *miser*.
The stingier you are, the more unhappy you will be. But if
you learn to trust God's promises and become big-hearted
and openhanded with what God has given you, you'll have
more joy than you ever imagined. If you want to be truly
happy, here is the guidebook."

Rick Warren, founder and senior pastor of Saddleback
Church and author of *The Purpose Driven Life*

"As I've gotten to know Ryan, I've been struck by how alive
God feels in both his life and his church. The principles in
this book explain why. I believe God will use *You of Little
Faith* to awaken and liberate many toward the kind of generosity that can radically change our lives, our churches,
and our world."

Todd Proctor, strategic church networks
director of Alpha USA

"This is a breathtaking—and necessary—book. Whenever
I hear or read Ryan teach on faith-based giving, I am filled
with courage and challenged to live into the kind of faith I've
always wanted—one that believes in a big God who can do
great things with small acts of faithfulness. Be prepared to
have your faith stirred by *You of Little Faith*—mine certainly
was in profound ways."

Drew Hyun, founding pastor of Hope Churches NYC

YOU OF
LITTLE
FAITH

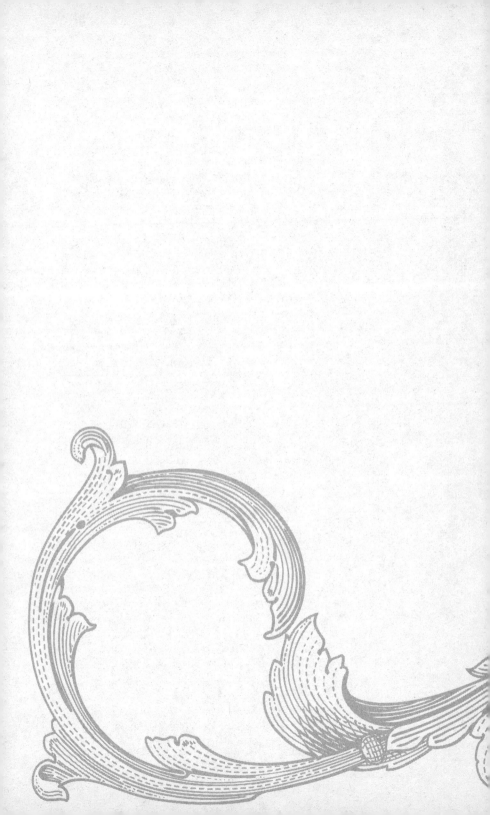

YOU OF LITTLE FAITH

How Bold Giving
Leads to Great Blessing

RYAN THOMAS

BakerBooks
a division of Baker Publishing Group
Grand Rapids, Michigan

© 2019 by Ryan Thomas Holladay

Published by Baker Books
a division of Baker Publishing Group
PO Box 6287, Grand Rapids, MI 49516-6287
www.bakerbooks.com

Printed in the United States of America

Library of Congress Cataloging-in-Publication Data
Names: Holladay, Ryan Thomas, 1984– author.
Title: You of little faith : how bold giving leads to great blessing / Ryan Thomas Holladay.
Description: Grand Rapids, MI : Baker Books, a division of Baker Publishing Group, [2019] | Includes bibliographical references.
Identifiers: LCCN 2019017849 | ISBN 9780801075056 (pbk. : alk. paper)
Subjects: LCSH: Christian giving. | Money—Religious aspects—Christianity.
Classification: LCC BV772 .H5825 2019 | DDC 248/.6—dc23
LC record available at https://lccn.loc.gov/2019017849

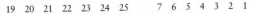
19 20 21 22 23 24 25   7 6 5 4 3 2 1

In keeping with biblical principles of creation stewardship, Baker Publishing Group advocates the responsible use of our natural resources. As a member of the Green Press Initiative, our company uses recycled paper when possible. The text paper of this book is composed in part of post-consumer waste.

green
press
INITIATIVE

This book is dedicated to the people of
LOWER MANHATTAN COMMUNITY CHURCH
whose willingness to risk and be rewarded
has grown my faith and given me joy

Contents

Contents

Introduction

This book is not about charitable giving. Not that I have anything against charitable giving—I just have very little interest in it. It's a subject I know next to nothing about, and it's something I have never participated in personally. Even as a pastor, not once have I asked our church to give charitably.

This book is about faith-based giving, which differs from charitable giving in three important ways.

FIRST, THE AMOUNT. Every year, most Americans participate in charitable giving of one sort or another. On average, they give around 3 percent of their income. This same rate applies to churchgoers. Christians in the United States give an average of 3 percent annually.[1] In other words, regardless of your religious beliefs, 3 percent is usually where charitable giving maxes out. There are obviously some outliers—the Bill Gateses and Warren Buffetts of the world who give far more because of their unique circumstances. But unless you're ultrarich or ultracompassionate, the ceiling for charitable giving is around 3 percent.

Faith-based giving, on the other hand, has a floor of 10 percent—more than three times the typical rate of charitable giving. And that's just a starting point. To really do it right, you've eventually got to go much higher. Which raises a question: Who in their right mind would do such a thing? That takes us to the next way faith-based giving differs from charitable giving.

SECOND, THE RECIPIENT. The obvious recipient of charitable giving is . . . a charity. Perhaps not always an official charity—the recipient could also be a charitable cause or a person in need. Regardless, the purpose of charitable giving is always the same: to help or to accomplish some good. You give because you believe that a particular person, organization, or cause needs your money and can benefit from it.

The recipient of faith-based giving is never a person, an organization, or a cause. With faith-based giving, you're giving your money to God.

For reasons we'll talk about later in the book, the simplest way of doing that is to give to your local church. But just because your giving goes to a church doesn't automatically qualify it as faith-based; it depends on your purpose. If your main concern is to support your church's particular programs—if you're mostly thinking about the good that will be accomplished and the people who will be helped—then your giving still falls into the charitable giving category. To truly qualify as faith-based giving, you must be giving *through* your church, not *to* your church. A faith-based giver gives to God, and only to God, and not because of how the money will be used. The church is just a proxy for God himself.

But why give to God in the first place? To state the obvious, God isn't needy. He doesn't want our charity; he doesn't depend on our money. Faith-based giving is never about helping God out. And, as we said above, it isn't about helping others out either. But this raises a puzzling question: If you're not trying to help God, and you're not focused on helping others, then who *are* you trying to help? The answer is surprising and at first offensive: in faith-based giving, the main person you're trying to help is you. That takes us to the final difference between these two types of giving.

THIRD, THE MOTIVES. Just as charitable giving is given *to* charities, it's also done *out of* charity. If you look up *charity* in the dictionary, you'll find words such as *generosity, altruism, philanthropy, benevolence,* and *compassion.* Charitable giving comes from the goodness of your own heart. It's selfless by definition; that's what makes it "charitable."

Faith-based giving comes from an entirely different place. It actually isn't selfless at all. One of the primary motives that drives faith-based giving is the pursuit of some reward—a reward so good that it puts you in an even better position than had you not given at all.

Many people know that Scripture promises rewards for giving, but they approach those rewards with an attitude of selflessness: "Well, if I happen to receive some reward as an extra bonus or side benefit, then fine. But that's not *why* I'm giving. The reward isn't what's motivating me; I'm certainly not seeking anything for myself." While that attitude sounds noble and mature, you won't find it in Scripture. Rather, when the Bible talks about giving, it's in terms of *consciously* seeking a blessing. A biblical giver says, "I'm giving *because* I want God to reward me. I wouldn't give nearly this much otherwise, and if I don't receive anything in return, I'll be severely disappointed."

If you're like most people, you probably think all that sounds backward. I've talked about this issue with a lot of people over the past decade, and I've found that almost everyone feels the same way: giving out of self-interest just feels *wrong*. Most of us have been taught that the whole point of giving is *not* to think about ourselves—if there's any selfishness mixed into our motives, it wipes out all the benefit of our action.

But what if that idea came from secular philosophers and not from the Bible? What if we're too noble, too mature, and too enlightened for our own good? What if giving from self-interested motives turns out to be *more* honoring to God and *more* beneficial to others than giving selflessly?

For now, the point isn't to convince you of anything I've said so far; the point is just to get the definitions clear. And they are as follows:

Charitable giving: when you give a small percentage of your income to help someone simply out of the goodness of your own heart.

Faith-based giving: when you give a large (and ever-increasing) percentage of your income to God because you want something from him in return.

If you're satisfied with the former, this probably isn't the book for you. But if you're intrigued by the latter, read on.

Our Story

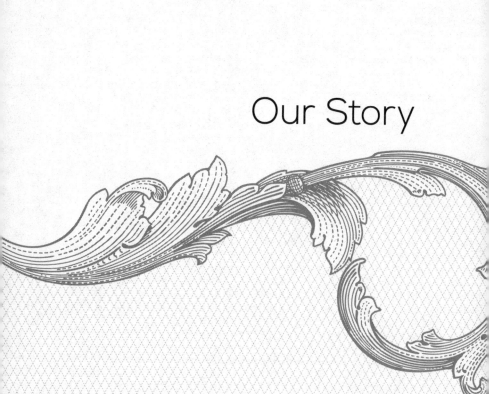

1

Decision

wo months after my wife, Brittany, and I were married, the church we were attending at the time began a giving campaign. Every family in the church was asked to make a commitment at the outset of the campaign, pledging the total amount they would give over the next eighteen months.

I was excited about this, because it was my first opportunity to try out faith-based giving for myself. Growing up, I had seen it modeled by my parents. I knew they always gave 20 percent of their income to our church as a matter of course. In addition, whenever there was a special offering, they sat us kids down and told us how much they were going to give. They explained that it would require some sacrifices, but they were trusting God to provide. And I had seen it work out. By the time I was a freshman in high school, my parents had given away my entire college savings. From a human perspective, this was foolish. But through unexpected channels, they received the same amount back (and more) during my senior year, just in time for me to attend private college—debt free.

Now that I was an adult, I felt it was my turn. Brittany and I sat down to talk about how much we would give over the next eighteen months. We both agreed that we wanted to give an aggressive, faith-stretching amount. We wanted to test God.

Before I tell you how much we decided to give, let me offer a disclaimer.

In the first part of this book—the first four chapters—I'm going to be sharing personal financial information. I have thought long and hard about whether to do this. The decision to include my own story in this book came only after a long struggle. There's a large part of me that doesn't want to share it—that is scared to. It makes me extremely uncomfortable for a couple of reasons.

First, I'm afraid I will be judged. I know that some readers will misunderstand and be turned off or strongly disagree—either with the actions we took or with my decision to disclose them. I'm even afraid of being judged by my own family and friends, many of whom I've never shared any of this with.

Second, I'm afraid of being praised. While some might condemn, others might applaud. To me, this second possibility is even more frightening. Jesus is very clear that as a general rule, we shouldn't tell others how much we give. He says that the praise we receive from others comes instead of the reward we might have received from God.[1] It's one or the other. By telling you about my giving, I'm sincerely afraid that I'll forfeit part of the reward. And I don't want that to happen.

But despite those two fears, and despite the fact that telling anyone how much you give is generally a bad practice, I still believe it's justified in some cases. And I think this is one of those cases. Here's why.

I've extensively reviewed my own motives, asking myself the question, *Why* do I feel that I should share this story? No individual is ever able to truly plumb the depths of their own heart, but as best as I can tell, my motive for wanting to share is this: I don't think you'll believe anything else I say in the rest of this book unless you know that I've tried this for myself. And I want you to believe the rest of this book. I want you to embrace faith-based giving. But if you don't know that I've tried it and seen it work, I don't think you'll really listen.

If that means I have to give up a share of my heavenly reward, so be it. Paul once said that he'd give up his own place in heaven if he could just convince his friends of the truth of the gospel.[2] The pastoral side of me feels somewhat similarly—I'd be willing to give up my own reward if I could convince you of how important faith-based giving is.

Another factor that convinced me to share my story was reflecting on how other people were willing to share their stories with me. I would never have understood the value of faith-based giving unless others had been willing to talk about it publicly and describe their own experiments. I would never have tried the experiment I'm about to describe had I not heard from others—others who were willing to be vulnerable and open themselves up to judgment and potential misunderstanding. So I feel it's my responsibility to pay it forward. If the vast majority of people who read this book judge me for it but a few are inspired to try it for themselves, I'd consider the trade well worth it.

Enough disclaimer. Back to the story.

BRITTANY AND I SAT DOWN to talk about how much we would give over the next eighteen months. We were both making about $35,000 a year at the time—a combined pretax income of around $70,000 a year. Over eighteen months we expected to make around $100,000. We decided to give half of that. Over the next year and a half, we pledged to give $50,000 to our church. Another way of looking at it is that, of our two salaries, we were pledging to give away one of them.

We calculated that we could maybe, almost, sort of, just barely get by on what would be left. It would be tight, but we could do it. We had a safety net of sorts. Entering our marriage, we had a combined savings of around $20,000. We were prepared to drain our savings if necessary. Because of this extra padding, our commitment of $50,000, though bold, didn't seem reckless or stupid.

One thing that was clear to me was that we were giving this money to God himself. The campaign was to raise funds for the construction of a new youth building. I don't get excited about buildings in general, and I certainly wasn't excited about this building in particular, at least not at the time. Up until then, the youth of our church had met in a large tent. I had grown up attending youth services in the tent. I loved the tent. I didn't see anything wrong with the tent. In fact, I preferred the tent to some shiny new building. I didn't see why the church needed to spend millions on a building when we already had a perfectly good tent.

So there I was, ready to give $50,000—half of our income—to a building I didn't even believe in. Why? Because we weren't giving the money to the building project. We weren't even giving the money to our church. We were giving the money to God. The church was just a conduit—the easiest, cleanest way I knew to give money straight to him. At the end of the day, it was the church leadership's job to decide how God wanted his money spent. They had prayed about that for years. I hadn't. They felt that this building would help our church to fulfill its mission. Who was I to argue? It wasn't my call. And it didn't really matter. To me, this was a covenant between God and us, and the church itself had very little to do with it.

FOR YOU TO UNDERSTAND the rest of this story—and for that matter, the rest of this book—it's important that I be painstakingly clear about exactly what our motives were in making this commitment. Just as important, it's crucial that I explain what our motives *were not*.

First, we weren't giving out of altruism—out of some sense that the church needed the money more than we did. Because that simply wasn't true. The truth was, we needed the money far more than the church did. Dollar for dollar, it would have had a far greater impact on our budget than on the church's budget.

Second, we weren't giving out of obedience. Yes, God had commanded us to give, but if we had been giving simply to fulfill his command, we would have given 10 percent, not 50 percent.

Third, we weren't even giving out of gratitude, at least not primarily. That's not to say we weren't grateful. We were. We were grateful for the way God had blessed our lives thus far. We were grateful for each other—that he had brought us together and allowed us to get married—and for so many other blessings and provisions. And, of course, we were grateful for all the "big stuff"—salvation and forgiveness and mercy and the cross. But gratitude, in and of itself, wasn't the thing that pushed us to give so aggressively.

Rather, one motive above all others caused us to give. The real reason we pledged to give as much as we did was out of self-interest: an expectation and desire for God to bless us in response.

We wanted a great life together. We wanted financial security. We wanted career advancement. We wanted children. We wanted influence and friends and a good reputation in our community. We wanted protection. We wanted favor.

In addition to all those tangible benefits, we also wanted the intangible spiritual benefits we knew would come with taking this sort of risk—a deeper faith, a greater sense of reliance on God, the peace that comes with not having to provide for ourselves financially, freedom from the bondage of materialism, the joy that comes with being generous, and the adrenaline rush that accompanies having to trust God. It's important to note that although the list of intangibles sounds somewhat spiritual, it's still selfish. It's still a list of things we wanted for ourselves. So although we gave *to* God, we gave *for* ourselves. We wanted God's blessing, and based on some of the promises in Scripture we had seen, as well as the testimony of people we trusted, we thought that trusting God with such an outrageous gift within our first three months of marriage had to be one of the surest ways to get it.

As it turns out, it was. Spoiler alert—it worked. God did bless us in response to our giving, beyond anything either of us had imagined. But it didn't happen the way we thought it would. Not even close.

2

Disappointment

In the previous chapter, I made a generic list of the types of blessings we were expecting in response to our giving that first year. But at the outset of the commitment, I also had some very specific ideas—some hunches—of how God might reward us. I had three ways in particular in mind that God might give back to us after we had given to him.

The first way was through a bonus. I was working for a small start-up at the time. Though my annual salary was only $35,000, there was an incentive structure built in, and I could earn bonuses of up to $50,000 based on performance. These were by no means guaranteed—in fact, they were something of a long shot. But still, the possibility was there. So my first thought as to how things would play out was that God would help me to earn $50,000 in bonuses, and we'd break even. In fact, the prospect of those bonuses was partly how we came to the $50,000 number to begin with.

The second way was through acceptance into law school. At the time, I had a half-finished seminary degree under my belt, but I had been wondering whether I was supposed to be a pastor after all. When I got married, I dropped out of seminary to work full-time and planned to apply to law school in the meantime. But as I wasn't sure this was what God wanted me to do either, I constructed a Gideon's-fleece scenario. I decided to apply to only one school: the University of Virginia. UVA is always ranked within the top ten law schools in the country. The problem was, I wasn't a top-ten applicant. The school had an extremely low acceptance rate, and my undergrad GPA was well below the average GPA that was admitted. But in looking at all the schools I could attend, UVA was the only school that stood out to me—that jumped off the page. So I reasoned, *If I apply to only this one school and I'm admitted even though it's clearly out of my league, that will be a sign that I'm supposed to go.* I submitted my long-shot application to UVA that November, the same exact month we started our giving commitment.

The third way I had in mind was through a book deal. The father of one of my friends from college worked for a large Christian publishing house. He knew I had tried my hand at writing, so as a kindness to me and without my asking, he had recently offered to show some of my work to various editors at his publisher. One of them liked what he saw well enough to begin working with me—unofficially, on the side—helping me put together something the publisher might want to acquire. I wanted this deal partly because of the financial component. Selling a book would help to recoup some of the $50,000 we were giving away. But I knew that a young, first-time author wouldn't get much of a first payment, an advance, on a book project, so it wasn't primarily about the money. It was more about the influence and opportunity.

FIFTY THOUSAND DOLLARS DIVIDED by eighteen comes to $2,777—a number I will never forget. To keep ourselves honest, we had decided at the outset of the campaign that for the next eighteen months, we would send in a check each month for $2,777, no matter what.

In January—three months into the commitment—the company I was working for folded altogether. Not only did I not have the opportunity to get the bonus, we also no longer had my salary.

That month, we sent in a check for $2,777.

After I lost my job, Brittany and I decided that perhaps it was a blessing in disguise and that I should work full-time on the book I had been trying to write. Which I did until March of that year—five months into the giving commitment—when I found out that the editor I had been working with was abruptly leaving the publishing industry altogether. I talked to a couple of other editors at the company, but they weren't interested. The book was dead.

That month, we sent in a check for $2,777.

Two of the three ways I had been anticipating God would bless us were now off the table. But there was still the prospect of me getting into UVA, which is where I put all my hopes.

In April of that year—six months into the commitment—I found out that UVA had rejected me. Logically, this wasn't surprising, but spiritually, it was devastating. I had convinced myself that this was something God wanted me to do and that he would make a way. I'll never forget getting the letter in the mail, telling Brittany, and watching the tears streak down her face.

That month, despite being 0 for 3 on rewards, we sent in a check for $2,777.

In my mind, this was now the absolute worst-case scenario. Not only had all three blessings failed to materialize, but I also didn't even have a job, which meant that we were at a crossroads. I didn't know it at the time, but the decisions we made at that juncture would shape the course of our lives for the next decade.

Our first option, and the most sensible by far, was to give up on the giving commitment altogether. We could chalk up the pledge to youthful exuberance and say we just got carried away and set the bar too high. In the first six months, we had already given $17,000, which was nothing to sneeze at. The most reasonable thing to do would have been to call it a day and admit, "Well, we tried, but this whole faith-based giving thing must not work the way we thought it did."

In talking and praying about it, however, we decided that this first option was a nonstarter for us. Less than a year into our marriage, were we really going to break a promise we had made to God? We determined that we'd finish the commitment of $50,000 even if it killed us. But how?

The most logical approach would have been for me to take the highest paying job I could find, regardless of whether the work was fulfilling. But there were three problems with this idea.

First, I had no marketable skills. I was a year out of college with no real work experience—a philosophy major with a half-finished seminary degree.

Second, I didn't feel that the giving commitment should be a trap. That's not how it was supposed to work. I didn't think God wanted it to be hanging over our heads, becoming something we resented. If I got a job that paid well but that I hated, I was essentially putting my life on hold for the sake of finishing the commitment. That didn't feel right.

Third, because we both had our hearts set on moving to Virginia for law school, we had been looking forward to the adventure of a cross-country move and living in a new place. Staying in California now somehow felt wrong. We wanted to move, and we didn't want to feel like the giving commitment was holding us back.

AS WE THOUGHT, TALKED, AND PRAYED, we finally decided on the following:

- It would be wrong for me to get a high-paying job that I hated just to "pay the bill" of the giving commitment. The giving commitment wasn't supposed to be a pair of handcuffs.

- Perhaps God hadn't allowed me to get into law school because he wanted me to finish my seminary degree instead.

- We should move somewhere else for me to attend seminary, trusting God to somehow (a) supply the money for us to complete the giving commitment, and (b) supply a new job for Brittany.

To us, pledging such a large amount was a step of faith. God was supposed to supply the money, not us. It would have taken the fun out of it—and changed the meaning of it—if we took matters into our own hands and seriously compromised our life plans just to keep the commitment. We wanted to trust God to work it out. He hadn't provided in the way we thought he might, but we were only six months into an eighteen-month commitment. There was still time. Who knew what he might do?

I started looking for a seminary to attend and found one in New York City—a dream location for both of us—that would take all of my transfer credits.

One upside of New York was that because of public transit, we could get rid of one of our two cars. Brittany's car was a newer SUV worth about $10,000. Mine was an old sedan, worth $1,500 on a good day. So we sold Brittany's car, thrilled that the proceeds would cover three and a half months of our pledge. We also sold all our furniture, putting the money aside for future giving installments. Next, we arranged to rent a three-hundred-square-foot furnished studio apartment in the nether regions of Manhattan. We hadn't seen pictures of it, or even a floor plan, but it was within walking distance of the seminary and the price was right—the cheapest thing we had seen. We signed a lease and hoped for the best. We couldn't afford a moving truck, so we got rid of most of our other possessions as well and packed whatever was left—all of our remaining earthly possessions—into the back of my 1990 Toyota Camry and hit the road.

3

Deliverance

Because we didn't want to pay for hotels on the cross-country drive from California to New York, we camped. When we reached Montana, we stayed in Yellowstone National Park, not only because we thought it might be our only opportunity to visit but also because it actually was cheaper than the KOAs we'd been staying at.

Our stop in Yellowstone fell over a weekend. That Sunday morning, we attended a service at a small church on the outskirts of the park. The sermon that day was on the importance of trusting God to provide materially and the futility of having too many possessions.

We could have patted ourselves on the back and thought, *There's one sermon we've got down already!* Instead, we were convicted. We went back to our campsite, took all our belongings out of the car and spread them out on a tarp we had laid down. Every possession we had besides the clothes on our backs was lying on that tarp. Then we asked ourselves which of them we could do without. We were able to let go of about half of what we still owned. We put it in bags and, on our way out of town, left it as a donation on the doorstep of the church we had attended—along with a note indicating that this was in response to the sermon. Everything fit much better in the Camry after that.

When we got to New York, we discovered that our apartment was marked with terrible odors (that wouldn't leave, no matter how many times we bleached the walls and floor). It was furnished with two twin beds instead of a queen. It was also infested with mice. I happen to have a full-blown phobia of mice. Still, we felt that it was God's provision and we were grateful for it—it was close to the school and affordable.

The next thing we needed God to provide was a job for Brittany. Like me, she had no working experience outside the church world, and her undergraduate degree was in Bible. This was a problem; it's not as though New York is a non-competitive hiring environment.

In other words, we really needed God to come through on this one. He hadn't blessed us the way we thought he was going to—through a bonus or a book deal or acceptance into law school—but we hadn't given up on him. So we prayed. And we reasoned with him and appealed to him on the basis of our commitment. We said, "God, we've promised to give you this money, but you have to do your part. You have to provide a job for Brittany. How can we give the money to you unless you first give it to us?"

It's important for you to understand the boldness with which we prayed this prayer. Our attitude wasn't "God, please-oh-pretty-please, take pity on us." It was rather,

"God, we're being faithful, so we expect you to be faithful. Do it."

As far as our part was concerned, we settled on a plan of attack. Brittany would apply for thirty jobs—the first thirty jobs she found online that looked like even remote possibilities. Then we wouldn't stress about it. We'd just trust with absolute certainty that God would come through.

These were all cold applications. We didn't have a single connection at any of the organizations. So you would expect that we wouldn't hear back from any of them. And we didn't . . . from twenty-nine of them. Brittany received a call from one and only one job out of all she had applied for. It was at Barnard College, an ivy-league women's school that's part of Columbia University. It happened to be two blocks from our house—the only job she had applied for that was in our neighborhood. (We had been prepared for the probability that she would have to commute up to an hour.) She was offered a job in their alumnae affairs department. Every other woman who worked in that office—every single one—was an alumna of Barnard. Brittany was the first nonalum that the office had ever hired. She had no business getting that job.

This was the first sign that maybe we were on to something after all, that maybe God would provide, and maybe it would all work out.

BRITTANY ALSO FOUND work as a part-time children's minister at a church on the other end of Manhattan. (Remember this church; it comes back into the story later.) She worked two jobs, and I found part-time work on top of going to school full-time.

Still, it was tight. With both of our lost work time and the expenses of the move, and with me working only part-time, we were cutting it very close. We reduced our expenses as much as possible, but our tiny, less-than-desirable studio was still costing us the same as our twelve-hundred-square-foot two-bedroom in California—$1,500 a month. Every month we were sending in a check to our church for nearly twice that. Every month, we would watch our savings dwindle even further.

As we drew nearer to the end of the commitment of eighteen months, it wasn't clear whether we were going to be able to complete it. We were prepared to take on credit-card debt if we needed to. But we didn't. The final month—April of 2008—we sent our final check for $2,777, bringing the total we had given to $50,000.

I'd like to say that we finished strong, but that wouldn't be true. It would be more accurate to say that we limped to the finish line. We had drained our entire savings. There was nothing left, and we were hardly going to be able to meet our expenses in the coming months.

What's more, I was going to finish my seminary degree in May of that year, and we had no plans of what to do next. I could get a job in the city, or we could move again. But at that point, it all seemed so arbitrary. Part of our expectation in making our giving commitment was that God would direct our lives. We were surrendering our path to him. Yes, he had prepared the way for us to come to New York, and yes, he had provided for us while there, but now what?

Suddenly, everything felt daunting. Not only were we financially drained from completing the commitment, we were emotionally and spiritually drained as well. We had been trying so hard to save that we just felt tired. One silly example: Brittany's hair dryer broke in January of that year, and she had decided not to buy a new one to save money. So every time she washed her hair, she would slick it back and put it in a pony tail, going to work with wet hair in the dead of winter. This wasn't logical; it was ridiculous. We should have spent the twenty dollars on a hair dryer, but we weren't thinking straight. In fact, studies show that the less money you have, the harder it is to spend it wisely.[1] We were worn down from trying to save, worn down from living with mice, worn down from sleeping on two twin beds put together. Somehow, even though we had completed the commitment, we still felt defeated. It was true that, against all odds, we had finished. We gave $50,000 away in our first eighteen months of marriage. But was this how it was supposed to go, with us having nothing left and no sense of direction? Was God really with us after all?

WHAT I HAVEN'T MENTIONED thus far is that the previous autumn, on first arriving in New York, I had reapplied to law school at UVA. This didn't make much sense. If they didn't want me the first time, they weren't going to want me the second. But I figured it didn't hurt to try; my application was already complete, so I just resubmitted it. I wasn't expecting anything—it's not like my GPA had gone up—but I thought, *Why not?*

In April of 2008, the month we finished our giving commitment—the exact same month we sent in our last check, fulfilled our promise to God, and proved to him that we were going to be faithful—I got a letter in the mail from UVA. It caught me off guard because I had completely forgotten that I had reapplied.

I opened it casually, thinking I'd find a second rejection letter. Instead, it said that I had been accepted. It also said that because I was in the top tier of applicants, they would like to offer me a merit-based scholarship.

The amount of the scholarship was $50,000.

Quick recap: same application as one year earlier, and they had turned me down flat. Now they were strongly asking me to come and offering me an amount that was exactly equal to the amount we had just given. It was probably a mistake on their part.

But not on God's part.

We moved to Virginia.

What you are starting to see, and what you'll see even more as the story continues, are two things beginning to merge: our giving and our lives. The giving commitment was now playing into our major decisions. God used it to direct us, to tell us, "This is where I want you to go next. I'm going to provide. Follow me here." But it was all intimately connected to our decision to give.

WHEN WE ARRIVED IN VIRGINIA, it was clear that God had once again gone ahead of us and paved the way. An apartment, friends, a job for Brittany, and a new church home all fell into place easily. We felt that we were right where he wanted us to be.

Still, there was an underlying tension. I loved law school, the debates, the close study of texts, the push for precision. But the more I learned about the actual *practice* of law, the more I struggled to see myself becoming a lawyer.

This left me confused. Why had God allowed me to get into a top school and provided a clear sign that I should attend with the $50,000 scholarship if this wasn't what I was supposed to do after all?

My thoughts returned to ministry. I couldn't make up my mind. While in seminary, I could dream of nothing but being in law school and wasn't able to imagine myself as a pastor. But now that I was in law school, I found myself thinking more about church work than about my legal studies. The pastor of the church we were attending in Virginia found out that I had been to seminary and asked me to fill in and give the sermon one Sunday in his absence. This led to him recommending me to other pastors in the area and to other invitations to preach. The weekend before final exams began the first semester, I found myself studying for a sermon I was about to deliver rather than studying for the exams. My heart was torn.

The one thing I felt certain of was that I could not leave the school. God had clearly led us there with the improbable acceptance and the $50,000 scholarship. We would not move until he told us to.

Which he did.

On Friday, February 20, of that first year at UVA—one month into the second semester—I woke up and turned on my computer to check my email. Brittany was still asleep; the house was quiet. There were two and only two messages in my inbox. Both emails were totally out of the blue from people I hadn't heard from or emailed with in quite some time. Just by the names, I was intrigued.

The first was from the pastor of the church we had attended during our year in New York, the church on the other side of Manhattan where Brittany had worked as a part-time children's minister. The email was short: two lines. It said that the church wasn't doing very well financially and that it was no longer able to pay a full-time minister's salary. The pastor had decided to look for a job at another church in order to better support his family. He asked if there was any chance I might want to move back to New York to take over the church for a minimal, part-time salary. It was either that or shut the church down completely.

THE PASTOR AND I HAD NEVER DISCUSSED anything along those lines before—not even the possibility. The thought had never crossed my mind, and I doubt it had ever crossed his until that week. But as soon as I heard his proposal, for some reason, my heart leapt. I had an immediate sense that this was meant to be. The church was small, seventy-five people or so. The pastor had founded the church himself. I was twenty-four years old and had never pastored before. Given those facts, I knew that half of the members would leave when the pastor left and that chances were the church would fold altogether within the first year. Yet I couldn't shake the impression that moving back to New York to take this job was what I was supposed to do.

But how would we support ourselves? We had already lived once in New York with no money and leaving had been

40

a tremendous relief. The thought of doing it again was less than attractive. What's more, how could I leave UVA when God had so clearly led us there?

That's when I opened the second email, which was from a relative. She said that she and her husband had been doing their estate planning and had decided to try something unconventional. Instead of leaving money to their family members when they died, they wanted to give it away while they were still living. She said they had always planned to leave something to me and Brittany and that they had decided now was the right time. She told me we'd be receiving a check—for $50,000.

Two and only two emails.

One that said, "Do you want to leave law school to try to take over a struggling church that can't pay your salary?"

And another that said, "Here's $50,000."

If you don't think that both of those emails are connected to one another, and if you don't think that both of them are connected to the original giving commitment we made several years prior, my question to you is, What would it take to convince you? What would you have to see before admitting that something was clearly God's miraculous provision? If something like this doesn't count, what would? Might your bar be set a bit too high?

4

Declaration

 accepted the job at the church in New York. Because the position was only part-time, we decided I would continue law school simultaneously. I put in transfer applications to the law schools at both NYU and Columbia, both of which are top-five schools, and neither of which I was qualified for based on my first-year grades at UVA. But at this point, do you really think I was worried about it? I was admitted to both.

As pastor of the church, I quickly determined that the first order of business was to make the church financially solvent. And that's when I began to see why God had sent *me*. The church needed to give, and I knew something about faith-based giving.

In November 2009, several months after we had arrived, I led the church in our first "Thanksgiving Offering." I proposed that we have a one-day offering in which we all gave a gift to God above and beyond our normal tithes. The purpose of the offering was to pay off some old church debts, buy some new equipment for the children's ministry, and send out a postcard announcing our Christmas Eve service. The goal for the offering was $25,000.

In 1 Chronicles 29, the Israelites were preparing to give a one-time offering for the building of God's temple. David, their leader, stood up and told the people exactly how much he himself was going to give toward the offering. The text says that the people rejoiced and were inspired by David's example. So I decided to do the same. I told the church that Brittany and I would be giving $5,000 toward the $25,000 goal, over and above our tithe. Brittany and I felt that the $50,000 we had just inherited was for two purposes: first, to get us through the lean years of the church's rebuilding phase, and second, to be given away.

When the day of the offering came, the gifts were totaled, and our tiny church (now having dwindled to about forty adults) had given $60,000 on a single day. This was equal to nearly half of the total annual giving at the church at that time.

And so it has gone for the last eight years. Every year, I have pushed our people to give more than they gave the year before, to trust, to sacrifice, to stretch themselves in faith, believing that God would bless them in response. Every year, they have responded. In 2010, my first full year at the church, total annual giving was around $200,000. In 2018, the most recent full year for which we have data at the time of writing, total giving was just over $3 million. That averages out to an increase of 40 percent per year in giving, whereas attendance increased only an average of 20 percent per year over that same period. In other words, giving has grown at a rate double that of attendance. Most churches see the opposite trend. Attendance may go up, but giving stays flat. But in our case, though our congregation is just over four times larger than it was eight years ago, we gave fifteen times more than we did then. Obviously, the only way to explain this is that the same people are giving more each year.

THROUGHOUT THIS PERIOD, I would never have dreamed of asking our people to give aggressively unless Brittany and I were willing to do the same. So every year we pushed ourselves to give an uncomfortable amount. Our faith-based giving was no longer a one-time, eighteen-month commitment that could be completed and put aside. It had become a way of life. In response to our initial $50,000 commitment, we had seen God give us back the same amount— not once but twice. We trusted that if we continued to give, we would continue to be rewarded.

And in some ways, we were. But in other ways, we were not. From the fall of 2009 through the fall of 2015, a six-year span, we had once again given well past $50,000, over and above our regular giving of 10 percent of our income. One way of looking at it is that we gave away the entire $50,000 inheritance, and then some. Just as God had given us the scholarship and then we let go of it so that we might follow him to New York, God had given us the inheritance and we were giving it back to him.

During those years, there's no question that God provided for us. The church was doing well financially. I was making a good salary. We eventually were able to move into a great apartment in a good neighborhood close to the church. But when the time came at the end of 2015 to make our giving commitment for the year ahead, we looked at our bank account and it wasn't a pretty picture. Because we had pushed ourselves to continue to increase our giving each year, we now found ourselves right back at the same place we had been at the end of our original eighteen-month $50,000 giving commitment back in 2008. We were once again broke. We had zero savings, zero retirement, and though we weren't quite living paycheck to paycheck, all of the money in our checking account was spoken for and would soon be gone. The worst part was that we had even been required to take on some low-interest debt to make ends meet. All of this because of what we had given. Had we given too much? Had we overdone it? Did the principle no longer work?

As the seventh giving season rolled around, we felt weary. Giving above and beyond our means for another year meant that, in all likelihood, we would go even deeper into debt. But we weren't ready to give up. And because I was asking our church to push themselves beyond what they had ever done before, how could we not do likewise?

So that November we again pledged to give a large amount over and above our tithe, not knowing where the money would come from.

In January, two months after the pledge, I got a call. Before I tell you who it was from and what it was about, I'll need to rewind a bit and bring you up to speed.

LET'S GO ALL THE WAY BACK to 2006 when we made the initial $50,000 pledge. You'll remember that, at first, none of the three specific ways I had been expecting God to provide panned out. But over the years, the picture had begun to change somewhat.

To review: The first way I had thought God might work was through a $50,000 bonus from the company I worked for. That didn't pan out initially. But three years later, we received the same amount—$50,000 in cash—in the form of the inheritance. So the exact thing I had been hoping for, breaking even on our giving commitment, came to fruition after all, just on a different timetable and through different means.

The second way I had anticipated God might work was through acceptance to UVA. Six months into our giving commitment, I was rejected. I considered this door closed. But then, in the final month of the commitment, I was accepted after all and with a $50,000 scholarship to boot. I had applied the first time during the same month we sent in our first check. I was accepted during the same month we sent in our last check, receiving back the exact amount we had given over the previous eighteen months.

But that still left the third way I had expected God might work back in 2006—the opportunity to write a book. You might remember that the only reason this was even a possibility at the time was because the father of one of my friends from college worked for a large Christian publishing house. When his publisher turned me down, I forgot about the idea of writing a book then and there. I made no efforts to write, whatsoever, in the intervening years. As far as I was concerned, it wasn't going to happen. But unbeknownst to me, my friend's father had continued to pitch me as a potential new author to literary agents he came into contact with—for ten years. I never asked him to do this. We never even corresponded about it during this time. He simply believed in me, decided that I was meant to write a book, and completely on his own initiative continued to pursue possible openings for me.

Finally, after nearly a decade, a literary agent actually took the bait and reached out to me. He asked me if I had any ideas for a book. I told him no. But I said I'd try to come up with something, and I wrote up a few ideas. He picked the concept he liked best and asked me to put together a two-chapter sample, which I did. He said he would take it from there, shopping it around to publishers. I didn't have high hopes. I was a first-time author with no track record and no platform, and honestly, though I believed in the concept, I didn't think the sample was very good. So in November of 2015, though I was aware that the agent was still shopping the sample around, it wasn't at all on my mind when we made our latest giving commitment. Besides, I had already heard from the agent that we had been rejected by a number of publishers, and I expected more of the same.

But in January of 2016, two months after our most recent commitment, the agent called and said we had received an offer. He admitted he was surprised at the amount of the advance. It didn't make sense for a first-time author with no platform and no track record. The advance they offered was $50,000.

Of course it didn't make sense, not on a human level. Just like it didn't make sense for UVA to offer me a $50,000 scholarship a year after they had rejected me, and just like it didn't make sense to receive a $50,000 inheritance from a living relative. But to Brittany and me, it made perfect sense.

The advance had nothing to do with the merits of my proposed book, just like the scholarship had nothing to do with the merits of my application. But they both had something to do with a certain commitment we had made back in 2006.

I KNOW THAT AN AUTHOR is not supposed to share the amount of a book advance. It's tacky, ill-mannered, and awkward. It took quite a bit of convincing to let my publisher even allow me to include that information. It's uncomfortable for them, and it's even more uncomfortable for me. I tried every way I could think of to avoid disclosing it. But ultimately, I had a choice to make: whether I was going to abide my normal standards of modesty and propriety, or tell you, in full detail, exactly how good and strong God really is.

I chose the latter, because I finally realized that God didn't drop this book deal in my lap, with almost zero effort on my part, just to give me $50,000 or to have the privilege of writing a book. Rather, he gave me the opportunity to write this book because there was something he wanted me to say, something he wanted me to tell you.

I struggled for over a year to figure out exactly what that something was. The book you are holding in your hands is not the book I originally proposed to the publisher. This isn't the book I had planned to write. I tried to write another book and failed. I don't know whether that book will ever see the light of day. What I do know is that finally, after over a year of trying to come up with something worthwhile from my own head, I heard God speak. This is what he said: "All you need to tell them in this book is the story of how you came to write this book. That's it. Tell them *this*. Tell them about how you met me face-to-face through the process of giving, and how they can do the same."

When God spoke to Moses from a burning bush and told him to go and lead the Israelites, Moses said, in so many words, "But what am I going to tell them?" To which God responded, "You can start by telling them about *this*. That you've met the living God."[1]

That's exactly how I felt on the day I got the letter from UVA, and on the day I received those two emails, and on the day I received the phone call from the agent.

That I had seen God.

IF SOMEONE WERE TO ASK me now, "Who do you think you are, writing a book? What makes you think you have anything to say? What are you going to tell people?" I would respond, "Well, I can at least tell you this. I can tell you how, over the past decade, I've experienced the type of relationship with God that I thought was only for people in the Bible. And all I had to do to embark on that journey was to give him the slightest signal: 'I believe your promises are true.'" That's what Brittany and I were doing when we pledged $50,000 as the first financial decision we made as a couple—just trying to send him a signal saying, "We're in. For whatever you have for us."

And God will not ignore that. He *can't* ignore it—he can't help himself. He is waiting, on pins and needles, holding his breath, ready to jump at the slightest indication on your part that you *actually believe his promises are true*. Second

Chronicles 16:9 says, "For the eyes of the LORD roam to and fro over all the earth, to show Himself strong on behalf of those whose heart is fully devoted to Him" (BSB).

And that's what giving is about. It's the best and the easiest way I know to say to God, "My heart is fully committed to you, and I'm ready for you to show yourself strong on my behalf."

Reward #1

Stronger Faith

5

Your Heart Follows Your Money

As a pastor, I frequently ask myself, *What's my job?* On one level, the answer is obvious: my job is to preach God's Word and serve his people. But when I ask myself this question, I'm trying to push a bit deeper and get somewhat more specific: *What is it, truly, that I'm trying to accomplish?*

I ask myself a similar question about the people who come to our church—not those who show up once or twice to check things out but those who come year after year. *Why do they come? What are they looking for? How can I help them?*

Over the years, through my own introspection and by talking to people in our congregation, I've discovered that there's actually a lot of alignment between the answers to those questions: my sense of what I should do is consistent with what those who come to the church are looking for. We both want the same thing.

And what we both want—what I want to do for them and what they would like me to do for them—is to push them spiritually. They want to be closer to God than they are. They want to have greater faith than they have. They want their lives to be richer, on a spiritual level, than they are. They ask things such as, "How can I feel and experience God more?" or "How do I get beyond learning and actually change?" They make comments like, "In my head, I believe. But in my heart, I can't feel it. It all makes sense, but I don't know how to make it more visceral and genuine. I want to bridge that gap."

I imagine you want those things too. That's the reason you picked up this book: you want to grow. So I'm going to make an assumption. I'm going to assume that my job with respect to you is the same as my job with respect to the people in my church: to try to move the dial in your life spiritually.

The reason I bring this up is because I want you to know where I'm coming from. There are parts of this book in which it may feel like I'm getting in your face, like I'm throwing down the gauntlet. It may feel as though I'm daring you and even being a bit mean. I don't intend to be mean, but I don't apologize for being direct. If it feels like I'm getting in your face, that's because I am. That's my job. To push you to be the person of faith that you say you want to be.

IF I'M GOING TO DO my job, and if my job is to help you grow in your faith, then there's one question that must be answered before any other: What does it take for a person to grow in faith? Once we've identified what change is needed in your life, it's then my role to do everything in my power to motivate you to make the change.

For example, if the job of athletic trainers is to help their clients grow their muscular tissue, they must start by asking, "What makes muscular tissue grow?" Once they figure that out, they then have to goad, coach, challenge, and motivate their clients to stretch those muscles in the ways that will cause muscular growth, even though their clients may not want to do it.

Do you see the irony? The reason people go to trainers in the first place is because they want the results. And they may even already know what would bring about those results. It's no mystery. But they don't want to lift the weights, run the miles, and do the exercises that will bring those results. So they need the trainer just to remind them over and over again: "You know, there's really only one way to do this."

And they say, "Are you sure there's only one way?"

And the trainer says, "Yep, there's only one way."

And they say, "OK. Here we go then. One more set."

The reason I love the topic of financial giving so much is because I have become convinced that it is one of if not *the* primary thing we can do to grow our faith. Giving works. Giving gets results. I have seen, time and time again, that this one discussion has the ability to create spiritual growth in a way that most other discussions do not.

Why? Because other discussions are exactly that: only discussions.

So much of our Christian practice is about words: words, words, words. We sing with words. The Bible is made up of words. Sermons are filled with words. We sit around someone's living room in small groups and try to put our thoughts and feelings into . . . words. For a lot of people, their entire relationship with God happens with their mouths.

But there's that great cliché, which couldn't be more perfectly applicable to this scenario: put your money where your mouth is.

And giving is one of the best ways I know of doing that. Literally. Because giving is an action. You're not just listening or processing or thinking. You're doing something very real with something that *is* very real: cold, hard cash. There's nothing academic about it. You're either in or you're out. And because it's an action, it moves the dial. It creates change.

So if you want me to help you grow your faith, giving is the one place we should start.

JUST AS WITH PHYSICAL TRAINING, most people are enamored with the idea of growing spiritually. But they are far less excited about the reality once they figure out what it actually involves.

If you say to me, "I want a stronger faith," I'll say, "Great. Let's talk about giving."

To which you might reply, "Oh. Money? Um, no . . . I think you misunderstood. I'm talking about spirituality. I'm talking about, you know, *faith*. Like the faith-in-my-heart type of faith. I was expecting you to tell me to read my Bible or pray or serve in a ministry. Something like that."

Of course, all of those things are wonderful and necessary. But they don't provide you with nearly as clear and straightforward an opportunity to exercise and build your faith as giving away your money does.

People are usually severely disappointed once they find out that this is what it comes down to. It's always been this way. There's a conversation in the Gospels when a wealthy young man comes to Jesus for the same reason you picked up this book: because he wants to be closer to God. And so he asks, "Jesus, what do I have to do? Teach me. Show me. How can I be a person of deeper faith? I know that's probably a super complicated question, and that there's probably not just one answer . . ."

And Jesus tells him it's not that complicated at all, and there *is* one answer. It's quite easy and straightforward. All he has to do is give his money away.

The Gospels say that, in response, the man "went away sad" (Mark 10:22). He wasn't angry or confused. He didn't argue or complain. He was just sad. Because that wasn't the answer he was expecting. He was ready to do anything but that.

A LOT OF PEOPLE HAVE this sneaking suspicion in the back of their minds that maybe church is just a scam, a racket. When they hear a pastor talk about money, that confirms their suspicion. You'll sometimes hear people complain, "All pastors want is your money."

But what I tell the people at our church is, "That's right. Guilty as charged. All I want is your money." Why? Because if I can get you to give away your money, then everything else will follow. That's what Jesus says in the Sermon on the Mount: "Where your treasure is, there your heart will be also" (Matt. 6:21).

We've heard this line so many times, we are no longer able to actually hear it. It sounds a bit like religious mumbo jumbo, and it passes in one ear and out the other. But just stop for a moment and listen carefully to what Jesus actually says. Listen specifically to the *order* of what he says, because the order matters. And most of all, listen to what he could have said but didn't. Because he could have said, "Where your heart is, there your treasure will be also."

If he had said *that*, then he would have simply been making an observation—offering a proverb of sorts. He would have been pointing out that as a general rule people tend to put their money into the things they care about. Which, of course, is true and somewhat insightful.

I suppose I could say something along the same lines to you. I could say, "If you really love God and if you really care about his kingdom, you will give as a result. Because where your heart is, there your treasure is also." That would be a true statement.

But that's *not* what I'm saying, because that's not what Jesus was saying. What Jesus was saying was much more profound and more interesting and more provocative than that. He doesn't say, "What you care about determines how you use your money." He says, "How you use your money determines what you care about."

This is an absolutely remarkable statement. If it's true (and, of course, it is—this is Jesus speaking), then it means that what we care about, what we feel emotionally connected to, is not out of our hands. It's not some deep mystery. Rather, it's entirely within our control. We can choose how we use our money, and our money is a lever that we can use to direct our own hearts.

This is outside-in thinking versus inside-out thinking. The Bible talks about both. We tend to mistakenly assume that spiritual growth always starts on the inside and works its way to the outside. But in this case, it doesn't. The way it works is not, "I wish I was more generous. I wish I had more faith. I wish I was closer to God. If I did, I would give." Rather, it's the reverse.

You don't become more generous, and then give.
You give, which makes you more generous.

You don't develop more faith, and then give.
You give, and it grows your faith.

You don't grow closer to God, and then give.
You give, and then start to feel closer to God.

Because where your treasure is,
there your heart will be also.

That's why this topic feels so life and death to me. I know that if I can just convince you to give aggressively, to give more than you ever dreamed possible and ever believed prudent, then from there, your journey of spiritual growth will largely take care of itself. I have seen life after life after life transformed by just taking this one simple step.

On the other hand, I know that if you don't give, there's very little I can do for you. Because God will never have your heart until he has your money.

6

Your Money
Represents Your Life

here's a fascinating exchange in Luke 3 between John the Baptist and the crowd he's preaching to. After he finishes, the people ask him a question: "What should we do then?" (v. 10). This is every preacher's all-time favorite question after a sermon. It means the sermon has landed. It's the exact same question the crowd asks Peter after his sermon on the day of Pentecost in Acts 2:37: "What shall we do?" And just before asking this, Acts says the people had been "cut to the heart."

That's why they're asking what they should do. Their hearts have been pierced, and they want to show it with their lives. So we can assume the same thing about John's hearers in Luke 3. They too have been cut to the heart. They've been convinced, and they want to repent and change. And so they ask John how.

John gives a different answer to three different groups of people who were there that day.

To the crowd in general, he says, "Anyone who has two shirts should share with the one who has none, and anyone who has food should do the same" (v. 11).

To the tax collectors, he says, "Don't collect any more than you are required to" (v. 13).

To the soldiers, he says, "Don't extort money and don't accuse people falsely—be content with your pay" (v. 14).

A quick, surface-level reading of this passage would tell us that the takeaway is that God's call on each person's life is different. Therefore, there is no one-size-fits-all approach to growing in faith. Three different groups of people, three different answers.

But a closer look reveals there's an element all three of these answers have in common. They all deal with money. The interesting thing is, no one had asked about money. They had asked about repentance—about salvation and baptism and conversion. But according to John, conversion and money seem to be inextricably linked. According to John, if you really want to know what it means to live a life that's connected to God, the first thing we need to talk about is your finances.

We see the same thing with Zacchaeus, another man who was cut to the heart. He too had a genuine conversion experience, but how can we tell? How does he indicate his changed life? Does he walk down an aisle or raise his hand or check a box on the back of a card or pray a prayer? No. The way Zacchaeus proves his conversion, the way he proves that it's *real* for him, is by giving. Luke 19:8 says, "But Zacchaeus stood up and said to the Lord, 'Look, Lord! Here and now I give half of my possessions to the poor, and if I have cheated anybody out of anything, I will pay back four times the amount.'"

That phrase Zacchaeus uses at the beginning of the verse, "Look, Lord!" reminds me of the way my girls say to me, "Dad, look!" They want me to see some new trick they've learned or project they've completed. They want me to be proud of them and impressed with them. It's the same thing with Zacchaeus. He has learned a new trick, and he wants Jesus to be proud and impressed. And Jesus is impressed. Upon seeing the gift, he says, "Today salvation has come to this house" (v. 9).

This lines up perfectly with what John the Baptist had said to the crowd. The people wondered how to prove they had turned their hearts to God, and John told them they prove it with their money. Zacchaeus could have said, "Jesus, look, I've really turned my heart toward God," and Jesus would have known it by what he did with his money.

ANOTHER WAY TO THINK about the centrality of money is to notice that no relationship is ever really serious until money is involved. This applies even to sacred, covenantal relationships. If you marry someone but you have a prenup to keep your finances completely separate, then it's fair to say you aren't truly married after all. You may be *legally* married but not spiritually, not on a soul level. Money is part of what seals the deal. Or, as another example, if you say, "I'm business partners with this person," but there's no money involved, then you actually *aren't* business partners. It's not serious.

It's the same with you and God. If money is not a major component of your relationship with him, then your relationship simply isn't serious. As long as the money belongs to you and he can't touch it, then everything with God is just a side thing—a hobby. It's something you do for fun, but it's not your real life.

Your real life is dollars and cents and careers and apartments and tuition and bills and loans and taxes and purchases and assets and liabilities and clothes and food. That's the serious, grown-up stuff.

If you don't give God your money, then you're essentially keeping him off to the side at the kids' table. But once he has your money, more of it than you can afford to let go of, all of a sudden you're playing for keeps. There's no distinction anymore between your real life on the one hand and your religious hobby on the other. Because now he's got something you care about—which means he's got you right where he wants you. He wants you to stop living life on your own and start living life with him. The best way he has of making that happen is to make sure you are tied up with him financially.

CONSIDER GENESIS 28 when God first calls Jacob. God appeared to him in a dream and said, in so many words, "Jacob, I'm choosing you. I'm going to bless you."

It's one of the holiest moments of Jacob's life, the moment when he first enters into a serious relationship with God. "When Jacob awoke from his sleep, he thought, 'Surely the LORD is in this place, and I was not aware of it.' He was

66

afraid and said, 'How awesome is this place! This is none other than the house of God; this is the gate of heaven'" (vv. 16–17).

And what is Jacob's response to all this holiness? God makes a pact with him, but how does Jacob feel that it's appropriate to seal the pact? To Jacob, it's obvious. There's only one real way to seal the deal—money. Genesis 28 continues:

> Then Jacob made a vow, saying, "If God will be with me and will watch over me on this journey I am taking and will give me food to eat and clothes to wear so that I return safely to my father's household, then the Lord will be my God and this stone that I have set up as a pillar will be God's house, and of all that you give me I will give you a tenth." (vv. 20–22)

What I love about this passage is the way it directly contradicts an attitude we sometimes come across: the feeling that money is almost *dirty*. I've discovered that one of the reasons people feel uncomfortable discussing money in church is because they think of money as being in this separate, nonspiritual category. They think of it as being a bit vulgar, almost like a necessary evil that should be talked about as little as possible. When someone starts talking about money in church, it can feel like a jarring mixture of the sacred and the profane.

This attitude, however, couldn't be more wrong. Look at Jacob. He has a holy, sacred experience, a pure and unadulterated encounter with God's presence, and his first thought is to bring money into it. Jacob understood the same principle that John the Baptist and Jesus both talked about: money is how you show that something is serious.

Money ups the stakes. Money makes it real. When you give God your money, you give him your life.

MOST PEOPLE WHO HAVE BEEN around church know that each of us is supposed to "give our life" to God. But how does that actually work? When Jesus says in Matthew 16:24, "Whoever wants to be my disciple must deny themselves and take up their cross and follow me," what does that mean in practice? For a small percentage of Christians, it means martyrdom, a literal laying down of their lives. But what about the rest of us? This is a universal command for everyone. There must be some way for *every* follower of Christ to "lay down their life." It can't be something reserved for a few special Christians.

The answer is straightforward: you lay down your life by laying down the things that make up your life. And what do we spend our lives doing? Trying to make, save, earn, invest, spend, not lose, and hold on to . . . money.

Our lives revolve around money.

It's true that our lives aren't about *just* money. Our lives also consist of our time, our energy, and our abilities. But that just about covers it. Those are the only four things we can give, in any context—our only four *assets*.

You might object, "But I can give my love!" But show me what giving your love looks like without giving any of the four things just listed. It isn't possible. Sort of like how James dares us to show our faith without action.[1] There's no such thing.

So the idea of giving God our love—and likewise, the idea of giving him our lives—is totally empty and meaningless unless we give him some real-world, measureable *thing*. Some asset that represents our love and our lives. And when it comes to the four assets we possess and could potentially give to God—time, energy, abilities, and money—I'm tired of people acting as if money is somehow less important than the other three. It's not. In fact, among these four assets, what's unique about money is that it can be a stand-in for the other three. Our money represents our *time* and our *energy* and our *abilities*, because we had to use those three things to get it. In that sense, our money might be the *best* proxy, the one that stands in for us, for our lives. If our money represents our time, our energy, and our abilities, then it represents *us*.

ONCE WE RECOGNIZE THIS, it puts everyone on a more even playing field when it comes to the biblical call to lay down our lives for Christ. Not everyone can be a missionary or a pastor or a social-justice worker. Not everyone can work in full-time ministry. But what does that mean in terms of heavenly reward? Does it mean that in the next life, all the pastors, missionaries, and nonprofit workers will get to go to the front of the line, while all the businesspeople will be considered second-class citizens since all they did was make a profit for their corporations?

The answer is no. Paul said to slaves in the first century, "Whatever you do, work at it with all your heart, as working for the Lord, not for human masters" (Col. 3:23).

For those slaves, this was just a mindset since they didn't receive wages. For people today, it's even easier to see the work you do for your company as "working for the Lord, not for human masters." Your company takes all the work you do, assigns a value to it, and gives it right back to you in the form of a paycheck. If you then turn around and give that money to God, you're no longer working for that company, you're working for God, because that's where your paycheck is ultimately going.

7

Faith Grows
When Stretched

 stated in the introduction that for faith-based giving to work, it requires giving an uncomfortable amount, giving until it hurts. If you don't give so much that your faith has to kick in, then your faith is not being stretched and you won't be guaranteed the rewards. There's a threshold you have to cross, a wire you have to trip.

In this chapter, I'd like to explore this concept in a bit more depth. Why does it work this way? What counts as an uncomfortable amount?

Ultimately, "uncomfortable" is a subjective standard based on how you feel. But we can flesh it out a bit. There are two numbers you can look at to determine whether you are truly giving away an uncomfortable percentage of your money. They are (1) the baseline percentage in Scripture, and (2) the percentage you have given in prior years.

THE BASELINE NUMBER GIVEN in Scripture is an easy one. The Bible gives us a place to start, and that number is 10 percent. Most people have heard of the concept of tithing. *Tithe* is just the old English word for tenth.

And you ask, "OK, but 10 percent of what?"

Well, 10 percent of everything. Ten percent of your total income, of your total yield for the year. And actually, if you've never given before, it would be 10 percent not only of your total income but also of your total assets for the years you weren't giving.

There are a few things to note about this number. First, 10 percent is *the* number. It comes up over and over again in the Bible in all sorts of contexts. It was recognized as *the* number for thousands of years by Jews, and it has since been recognized as *the* number for thousands of years by Christians. So it's not like there's any debate about it: "Maybe it's 5 percent, or maybe 20 percent." No, 10 percent is the baseline number.

Second, when I say 10 percent is the baseline, what's important to understand is that this is a floor, not a ceiling. What the New Testament makes clear is that as we grow in our faith, God expects us to work toward giving away far more than 10 percent—something we'll talk about shortly. Some passages in the New Testament reference 50 percent or 100 percent. So 10 percent is where you start, and you grow from there. But you grow *from* there, not *to* there.

You don't say, "I'll start at 1 percent and gradually increase to 10 percent." That's not how it works. Ten percent is the minimum.

Third, this number is a rule of thumb, not a law. It actually *was* a law for a time in the history of Israel. But the guideline and practice of giving 10 percent existed *before* it was ever a law. In Genesis, we see both Abraham and Jacob, on separate occasions, giving 10 percent of their total income even though it was not legally required. So just as this rule of thumb existed before the law was written, so too it exists after the law no longer applies.

By saying it's a rule of thumb and not a law, what I don't mean is to feel free to ignore it. What I mean is don't forget that this rule is there for your benefit, for your convenience. To try to get around it is just shooting yourself in the foot, assuming, of course, your goal is to receive the blessings and benefits of giving that are described in Scripture and outlined in this book. If you want those things, then there's no point in giving less than 10 percent, because less than 10 percent isn't enough to stretch your faith and trigger the reward.

If you're giving for some other reason—for example, out of altruism or a sense of duty or gratitude—then feel free to give as little as you please. This goes back to the discussion of charitable giving in the introduction. The whole idea of charitable giving is that you give just for the sake of giving, out of the goodness of your heart. As we talked about already, most Americans engage in this sort of giving. Even if they just give five dollars to the Red Cross, one dollar to a homeless person, or drop a twenty-dollar bill in the plate at church, it warms their heart a bit and reduces their guilt.

That's charitable giving. And if you want to be a charitable giver, then by all means, give as little as you please.

But faith-based giving is about giving more, because you're after something and you want to make sure you get it. For this type of giving, the floor, the absolute minimum, is 10 percent of your total income.

WHAT PEOPLE ALWAYS WANT to know next is whether it's 10 percent before tax or 10 percent after tax. The answer is before tax.

If you give God 10 percent of what's left over *after* you pay the government, then what you're doing is putting the government in line ahead of God.

You might object, "But I don't have a choice whether to pay taxes." That's true. But there are all kinds of expenses in which you don't have a choice. You don't have a choice whether to pay your electric bill either.

So what's so different about the money you pay in taxes versus your other bills? Is it just that it's taken out of your paycheck before you actually see your check? But that's nothing more than automatic bill pay, something your company does as a convenience to you. It's still *your money* that's being paid out. Taxes are no different from any other mandatory expense.

If you say, "I'm gonna pay my tax bill first, and then re-calculate and give 10 percent of what's left after that," my response would be, "OK, but if God's going to go second, why not have him go third or fourth? Why not subtract taxes *and* utilities *and* groceries *and* rent *and* tuition *and* your retirement contribution and then give God 10 percent of what's left after that?"

All of this goes back to the idea that the tithe is a rule of thumb, not a law. If it's a law, then you should try to figure out ways around it, to circumvent it. Which is what people do with the tax code. But if it's a rule of thumb and not a law, then you've got to remember that nobody is making you do this. The rule is to help *you.* After all, why did you go asking about the rule in the first place? You could have not asked what the rule of thumb was and just given whatever you felt like. But the reason you asked is because by giving whatever you feel like, *you run the risk of giving too little*—which is what you wanted to avoid. But don't you see that you run the exact same risk, you put yourself at risk of giving too little, by reinterpreting the rule and putting your own spin on it?

So that's where faith-based giving has to begin: 10 percent of your total pretax income. To someone who is currently giving less than that, I would say, start there. My bet is that if 10 percent feels plenty uncomfortable for you, which is good, that means it's large enough to trip the wire and bring the reward.

WHAT ABOUT THOSE WHO ARE already giving 10 percent?

Let's go back to the analogy of athletic training we talked about in the first chapter of this part. In strength training, there's a principle called progressive overload, which says that the only way to grow a muscle is to progressively place a higher and higher load on it.

If you saw my physique, you'd know immediately that I haven't ever personally applied this principle in the gym. But where I have applied it, and where it works the same way, is on a spiritual level.

How do you make sure that giving keeps working for you? How do you ensure that it continues to grow your faith and bring the promised rewards?

The answer is to keep giving more. It's not enough to continue to give. You've got to give more each year than you've ever given before—not in terms of the absolute dollar amount but in terms of the percentage of your income. Because faith is a muscle, and the only way to grow it is to push it harder. By giving more than you gave in the past, you're picking up heavier and heavier weights, and your faith will get bigger and stronger as a result. Progressive overload.

So you start at 10 percent, and you think, *There's no way. There's just no way I can give God 10 percent this next year. I can't do it, but I'm gonna try anyway.* And what will happen is you'll find out that you *can* do it. God will supply your needs, as it says in Philippians 4:19. You'll test God, and he'll come through, as it says in Malachi 3:10. You just did something you didn't think you could do. In the process, you found out that God could do something you didn't think *he* could do. It was scary, you jumped, and he caught you. As a result, your faith is now stronger. You've got bigger faith muscles than you had before.

What's next? If you keep giving 10 percent, it's just maintenance. It's never going to do the same thing it did that first year. Because you already know you can give 10 percent and God will meet your needs. That doesn't feel impossible anymore. There's no strain. If you keep lifting the same weight, it doesn't matter how faithful and consistent you are to your workout schedule, your muscles will not grow. It's the same thing with faith. To keep your faith growing, you have to keep doing what feels impossible. You have to keep pushing yourself to keep creating the feeling of "God certainly can't supply my needs if I give X; that's too much." And then you do. And then he does.

The easiest way to do this is to start upping your giving by a small percentage every year. Even if it's just 1 percent or maybe 2 percent or 5 percent—however bold you feel. Let's say you gave 20 percent of your total income away last year. Just decide, "This year, we're gonna try to give 22 percent." And you make it a goal to play this game with God to see if you can keep doing this year after year. You can even set a goal for decades out. For example, "By the time we're 50, we want to be giving 50 percent away." I know of couples who in their twenties started this game at 10 percent, saying, "We're going to up it every year, no matter what," and by the time they got to their fifties they were giving 90 percent away. That's reverse tithing: living on 10 percent and giving 90 percent back to God.

YOU MIGHT ASK, "But why should I care? Why should I care if I get bigger faith muscles? Big deal. I can't even show those off at the beach." Which, of course, is why most people work out today, because they want to look good. There's nothing wrong with that. But because this motivation is so common, we've almost forgotten that there are people who lift weights for other reasons.

Think about athletes and soldiers. They don't go to the gym because they want a six-pack. They go because the harder they push themselves there, the more they're able to do out on the field—the playing field or the battlefield.

In that case, going to the gym is like a simulator. It's fake. You are choosing to place yourself under artificial strain, willingly bringing hardship and difficulty into your life. There is no real enemy, no true opponent, and no actual fight. You just simulate an opponent using heavy metal plates. But if you push yourself, and do it in a thoughtful way, it prepares you to handle actual battle.

Giving works in the same way. Giving is the gymnasium of faith. When you say, "I'm going to give X this year," when you push and stretch yourself, you're choosing to create artificial hardship in your life. You're choosing to strain yourself and are voluntarily bringing a certain amount of pain and suffering and stress into your life. Why? Because it prepares you for game day. As you take risks with God financially and your faith grows as a result, you've gained the confidence in him to take risks in other areas of your life. You're ready to do big stuff for him in the real world, because you've bulked up in the gymnasium of faith.

On the other hand, if you don't give aggressively, if you don't push yourself in this area, you'll remain a weakling in faith. God still loves you but he can't do much with you, because you haven't learned to trust him.

8

There Is No Faith without Action

To truly understand how giving strengthens our faith, it's worth pausing to clarify a fundamental question: What exactly *is* faith, anyway? It may be one of the most misunderstood and misused terms in all of Christianity.

Let's start by identifying some things that faith is *not*.

First of all, faith is not the same thing as believing in God. These two things are commonly mixed up, but they're completely different. The authors of Scripture go out of their way to distinguish them. James writes sarcastically, "You believe that there is one God. Good! Even the demons believe that—and shudder" (James 2:19). James would say that believing just puts you on par with the devil. That's certainly not equivalent to true faith.

Second and closely related, faith is not a catchall term for our relationship with God or for our religious/spiritual life in general. This is the most common way the word *faith* is misused. When someone says, "My faith is very important to me," they often simply mean, "I'm very religious." When someone says, "I wish I had stronger faith," they usually just mean, "I wish I went to church more." There's even that phrase "a person of faith," which for most people is again just another way of saying "a religious person."

Those are all very sloppy usages of the word. True faith is not synonymous with religion or having a relationship with God in general. Rather, faith is one distinct *part* of our relationship with God. It's one of many components. These components can't necessarily be separated, but they can still be talked about distinctly.

The most important component of our relationship with God is love. It's even more important than faith. But right *under* love in the hierarchy of what matters in this world, and what matters in the world to come, and what matters to God—the second most important thing in the universe, you might say—is faith.

So what is faith?

I'D LIKE TO SUGGEST a very simple definition. Faith is

taking an action
based on the assumed truth
of something God has said.

First, faith is *taking an action*. It's important to be clear on this point. Faith is always an action. It's not merely cognitive, emotional, or internal; it's an external action in the real world. If there's no action, there's no faith. Though one of the three great "solas" of the Reformation was the idea that we are saved by "faith alone," the Reformers themselves were quick to admit that "faith alone" isn't truly faith at all.[1] James makes fun of people who claim faith is an internal thing. He tries to show how ludicrous this is by suggesting an experiment: "Show me your faith *without* deeds, and I will show you my faith *by* my deeds" (James 2:18, emphasis added). His point is, you can't show faith without action because faith *is* action.

But what sort of action? That takes us to the next two lines in the definition: faith is taking an action *based on the assumed truth of something God has said.*

Before we look at how this works with respect to God, let's first note that this is what faith means in any relationship. If we act based on the assumed truth of something someone has said, we are placing our faith in them. For example, if you tell me that we're going to meet at 1:00 p.m., and I start walking confidently to our meeting place, that action equals faith. I'm assuming what you've said is true. Alternatively, I might decide to leave a little bit late, because I know you have a tendency to be late. In other words, in that instance I *don't have faith in you.* You've said you're going to be there at 1:00 p.m., but I'm not certain enough of the truth of that statement to take action based on it.

Faith in God works in the same way. Faith is taking an action based on the assumed truth of something God says. And in the Bible, he says a lot of things. Some he says to specific people, and others are intended for everyone. Many of the things he says are if-then statements or statements about the future. For example, he might say, "If you do X, I'll do Y" or "Because A is going to happen, I suggest that you do B."

What I've found from experience is that many people most of the time hear what God says but think, *I bet that's not true. I bet it won't happen the way he says it's going to happen* or *I bet he won't hold up his end of the deal, even if I hold up mine.*

The heroes of faith in Scripture are simply those rare people who think the opposite. They hear God's statements and think, *You know, if that's true, and I assume that it is, then the only rational thing for me to do is* . . . And then they take an action based on that assumption.

Hebrews 11 is known as the Faith Hall of Fame, and it gives example after example of such individuals.

Noah had faith. He took an action, built a giant boat, assuming the truth of what God had said—that a huge flood was coming.

Abraham had faith. He left his homeland, giving up all his comfort and security, assuming the truth of what God had said—that if Abraham did as he was told, he would become even more wealthy, even more secure, and would be the leader of a great nation.

Moses had faith. He gave up his position in Pharaoh's court, risking his life and enduring all kinds of hardships to lead the Israelites out of slavery, assuming the truth of what God had said—that the rewards of the promised land would be greater than the rewards of Egypt.

That's faith. That's all it is: taking an action based on the assumed truth of something God has said.

NOW THAT WE'VE GOT the definition down, there are two points worth noting about faith, two ways that true faith is completely different from so-called faith as we typically talk about it.

First, notice that actions of faith are totally *rational* so long as our assumption about the truth of what God has said is correct.

I bring this up because we sometimes see faith pitted *against* reason. People will talk as though faith means doing something crazy, taking some irrational leap, whereas reason means doing the thing that is safe and seems prudent. They'll say that we sometimes act contrary to reason, that we're called to obey God "even when it doesn't make sense."

That's an extremely unhelpful and misleading way of construing things. This is how it really works: God states, "Do this, and that will happen." Because it's a statement about the future, there's no way for anyone to know for sure if it is true. Yet we all have to decide whether to act on it based on whether we *think* it's true.

For example, if a financial analyst on TV says, "This stock is going to go up 20 percent in the next two weeks," you have two options. You can either put your faith in him and buy more of the stock because you think, *Yeah, he's probably right*, or you can *not* put your faith in him and not buy more of the stock because you think, *No, I don't think he's right*. Both actions are equally rational; they're both actions consistent with your premise.

So it is with God. If you assume what he says *isn't* true, even though you can't know for sure, the only rational course of action is to ignore it. On the other hand, if you assume what he says *is* true, even though you can't know for sure, the only rational course of action is to follow it. So not only are actions based on faith or lack of faith equally rational—they're also equally risky. They are equally a "leap" of faith because you're placing a bet either way, and either way, you could be wrong.

If you act as though God was telling the truth, but he wasn't, then you're going to fall flat on your face. But if you act as though he wasn't telling the truth, and he was, the consequences could be much worse. If Noah had built the boat and the flood had never come, he would have wasted his life. But if Noah hadn't built the boat, he would have lost his life. He was betting his life either way.

The second interesting feature to note about true faith is that all the examples of faith given in Hebrews 11 are self-serving.

Again, this goes against the way we usually talk about faith. People often think faith means disregarding our own self-interests because we're "doing the right thing" or obeying God, whereas lack of faith is looking out for and protecting and preserving ourselves.

But if you look at Hebrews 11, you'll see that acting on faith does not mean disregarding one's self-interests. Someone steps out in faith. And that individual reaches their goal. In the process, God never says, "Do this; it's going to be awful but do it anyway because I'm God." Rather, it's as if he says, "Do this, and if you do, it's going to work out better for you than if you hadn't."

Scripture is very honest about these self-serving motives on the part of the great saints. What drove Noah to build the ark? "In holy fear [he] built an ark to save his family" (v. 7). Why was Abraham willing to live in tents? Because "he was looking forward to the city with foundations" (v. 10). Why was Moses willing to leave the comfort of the palace? "He regarded disgrace for the sake of Christ as of greater value than the treasures of Egypt, because he was looking ahead to his reward" (v. 26).

Do you know what it's called when you are willing to pay the price because you judge the reward to be of greater value? It's called cost-benefit analysis. And there's nothing particularly noble about it.

That's all faith is. True faith is cost-benefit analysis. It isn't altruistic, and it isn't even necessarily dutiful. It's doing what you think is best for you, assuming the intel you have from God is accurate. It always takes into account your own self-interest and well-being. You're placing a bet by taking an action. Because faith is simply taking an action based on the assumed truth of something God has said.

But all of this still leaves open a question: What does any of it have to do with giving?

9

Giving Is the Perfect Test of Faith

he purpose of the last chapter was to define faith with more accuracy and more precision. Now that we're equipped with a better definition, how does it apply to our lives?

First though, after reading the previous chapter, I'm concerned someone might be thinking something along these lines: *Well, now I understand what faith is. But I'm not too worried about it, because it seems somewhat like extra credit, like something for special people in special circumstances. After all, there's a Faith Hall of Fame in Hebrews. I don't necessarily aspire to be inducted into it. So faith is sort of a heroic thing that a few top-tier believers might be called to exercise a few times in their lives.*

That understanding would be mistaken, because Hebrews 11:6 tells us, "Without faith, it's impossible to please God."

In other words, faith is crucial for everyone. We can't have a functioning relationship with God *at all* unless we're living by faith. And remember, we're not talking about faith in the vague, generic sense in which people usually use the term—a catchall way of talking about a relationship with God. We're talking about faith according to the specific definition outlined in the previous chapter—an action based on what God has said. If it's impossible to please God without faith, and if faith is taking an action based on the assumed truth of something God has said, do you see what putting those two things together means for us? It means that if we aren't acting on the truth of God's statements, we aren't living a life of faith and our life isn't pleasing to God.

You might say in response: "But God hasn't told me to do anything. He hasn't made any statements that I can assume are true and that I can act on. He hasn't told me a flood is coming. He hasn't told me that he'll bless me if I leave my home and move. He hasn't asked me to leave the palace and free the slaves. There's no promise or command that's been issued to me. So I'm off the hook, because how can I be expected to do something if there hasn't even been an opportunity?"

I suspect a lot of people feel that way. They're actively trying to be spiritual people and to have some sort of relationship with God, but they are not living a life of faith in the true sense of the word. They're still waiting for God to call their number. In the meantime, they're sitting on the sidelines of the faith game, just watching.

The Bible, however, is full of promises and commands from God to us, universal promises and commands for everyone. I don't mean verses that you read and think, *Does*

this apply to me? It says, "Moses went up the mountain."
Should I go up a mountain? I'm talking about commands
and promises that are unambiguously universal.

They are everywhere in Scripture. It's up to each of us to
decide whether we're going to act in light of them. If they're
true, the only smart thing to do, even just from a selfish
perspective, is to act on them. If they're not true, the only
smart thing to do is to ignore them. We each have to decide.

THIS IS WHERE GIVING COMES IN. The reason I love
the topic of giving so much is because giving is the area in
which some of God's clearest, most direct, and most applicable commands and promises are found. It's one of the most
notable examples of an area in which God has already called
your number. He has issued a universal invitation that's easy
to understand. *And attached to it is a promise that is in your
own self-interest.* God says, in effect:

> Here's what I want you to do. I want you to give your money
> to me, even to the point of disregarding your own material
> needs. Give more than you feel you can afford to give. How-
> ever much you've given before, give more than that.
>
> And if you do that, two things will happen.
>
> First, I will bless you materially in this life. I will give back
> to you, in kind, with actual money, and will take care of your
> needs better than you could take care of them yourself. I will
> open doors and opportunities and bless your career.
>
> Second, I will also bless you in the next life, in proportion
> to the amount you gave. You will have wealth in the world

to come, treasure in heaven, in direct proportion to how aggressively you gave in this life.

You might ask, "Does God really say that in the Bible? All of that?"

Yes, he really does. In the rest of this book, we're going to look at the passages of Scripture that back all of that up. But for now, just assume I'm telling the truth. If the Bible really does say that, if God really does issue that command and attach those promises, do you see how this is a textbook faith scenario? Do you see how this is your chance, your test?

It's all there in black and white: the Word of God to you. It's an if-then statement, a command coupled with a promise about how things will be in the future if you abide by it. This is the perfect setup for anyone and everyone who desires to dip their toe into the waters of faith.

This is your opportunity to discover if you have true faith. Because if you assume that what God said is true, then you'll do it. No question. It would be stupid not to. This means that if you're not doing it, the only possible explanation is that you assume it's not true. You don't have faith. You may have something else—belief in God or some sort of religious feeling or sentiment—but not faith.

DESPITE WHAT WE READ in the previous chapter—that the heroes of faith in Scripture were motivated by self-interest—I find that people are hung up on the thought that we are to consciously seek God's blessing through our obedience. They ask me, incredulously, "Are you saying that my motive in giving should be because I'm seeking a reward? That I should be giving *because* I want God to bless me and take care of me?"

Yes, that's exactly what I'm saying. Let me put an even finer point on it. If you give to God because you want him to bless you in return—take care of you on earth and give you treasure in heaven—that motivation is, in fact, higher, purer, and more God-honoring than giving out of the goodness of your heart.

Why? *Because selfish giving is the only type of giving that really depends on faith.* Every other type of giving can be done without any real faith at all.

Many people say, "I don't care if God blesses me in response. That's not why I'm doing it. If I get a reward, fine, but I'm not doing it for the reward." But you know what I think? I think it's not that you don't care whether he blesses you, it's that *you don't think he can or will.* You don't believe. What's parading as spiritual maturity is really nothing more than doubt in disguise.

People will sometimes say, "I would be a Christian even if there were no heaven." When Paul heard this from the Corinthians, he flew off the handle and said, in essence, "That's the dumbest thing I've ever heard. If we do all this and there's no reward at the end, then we're pathetic."[1]

We've been trained to think that the focus of our belief should be on God himself and not his gifts and blessings. But let's go back to Hebrews 11:6 and break it down:

> Without faith it is impossible to please God,
> because anyone who comes to him must believe that
>   he exists

and

that he rewards those who earnestly seek him.

The last clause is part of faith. Faith isn't only believing in God. It's also believing that God will reward us if we seek him. If we just believe in God and don't believe that he rewards, then we don't have faith at all.

The problem with believing only in God himself and not in the fact that he will do some specific thing for you is that it always leaves you an out. You say, "I believe God can, in theory, move mountains," but you never ask him to move *your* mountains. Your faith is never put to the test—it's purely academic and can never be disproved. There is no risk.

There *is* a risk when you seek a reward. The risk is this: if the reward is not given, you've made a fool of yourself and done it all for nothing. As Paul said, if there's no heaven, we've wasted our lives. And I'd say the same thing about the rewards of giving. If you give, and you don't get what God promised in return, then you simply wasted your money.

Counterintuitively, this means we need to flip our normal motivational hierarchy on its head. We should do things for the "right" reason, but the right reason is the exact opposite of what we've already assumed. We think that the right reason means we do things from selfless motives, and the more selfless the better. But the surprising truth is that seeking the reward for ourselves is actually the higher motivation—the more holy one. It's *better* to follow God because of what we're going to get in return, instead of following him just because he's God.

Why? Because if you do something for a reward, it proves that you believe there actually is one. You believe that God can change events and people's lives in the real world. You're factoring him into your plans, which is what he wants. The advertised rewards are a test. The rewards aren't a side benefit; they are the whole point. Because God is searching to and fro through the whole earth, looking for whose who believe that his promises are true.

Reward #2

Freedom
from Materialism

10

More Is Never Enough

Why is giving such a big deal? Why is giving so powerful?

We've already seen the first answer to these questions: giving builds your faith like nothing else can, because when you give God your money, you give him your life.

In the next three chapters, we're going to look at a second reason giving is so spiritually powerful and life transforming: giving is the solution to the primary spiritual issue of our day—materialism.

Materialism has been called a philosophy or even a disease. But it's more accurate to think of it as something else. Materialism is nothing less than a full-blown religion.

It's by far the most widely practiced religion in New York City where I pastor. The vast majority of New Yorkers are devout materialists. New York is arguably the world headquarters of the Church of Materialism. But materialism is also the most widely practiced religion in Southern California where I grew up. So it's the most popular religion on both coasts, and the same is true for much of the rest of the country.

TO HAVE A RELIGION, you need some doctrines. What do materialists believe? There are three main tenets of materialism—three doctrinal pillars—which are as follows:

If I have more, then I'll be happy.
If I have more, then I'll be safe.
If I have more, then my life will matter.

To put these same three beliefs in slightly different language, materialism teaches that:

More money will bring me satisfaction.
More money will bring me security.
More money will bring me significance.

No one, of course, admits to believing those things. No one actually says them out loud. Most people don't even realize they believe them. But, in fact, the vast majority of Americans do subscribe to these three ideas. If I'm right, it would explain everyone's constant, unending push for *more*. These three underlying beliefs are the only way of making sense of why we all practice this secret religion.

What's interesting about materialism is that everyone can easily see its influence in the lives of others, but hardly anyone can see it in themselves. You know plenty of people who have and make and spend more than you do. You think, *Sure, they're materialistic. But not me.*

In Luke 12:15, a man comes to Jesus and says, "Teacher, tell my brother to divide our parents' estate with me." This seems like a reasonable request. But Jesus responds, "Watch out! Be on your guard against all kinds of greed." Jesus doesn't say "Watch out!" too often. The implication is that *you can be greedy and not know it.* In fact, you almost never know it.

Greed is one of the seven deadly sins. But compare it to some of the other sins on that list—lust, anger, and envy, for example. As a pastor, I've had people come and confess that they are struggling with lust. I've had people come and confess they are struggling with anger. I've had people come and confess they are struggling with envy. But I have never once had anyone come and confess to me that they are struggling with greed. The only people who have ever confessed greed are those who have somehow broken free from it and, looking back, can see it.

SO JESUS SAYS TO WATCH OUT because life does not consist of the accumulation of things. In other words, more is not the answer. More won't make you happy; more won't make you safe; more won't make you matter.

In response you might say, "I already know that." If that's true, then let me ask you a question: Why do you still want more?

You might answer, "I don't want *more*; I just want enough."

Fine, but then tell me this: Why does the bar for *enough* keep moving? Because what you have now *was* your definition of *enough* ten years ago. But somehow it's not enough anymore. And as for your current definition of *enough*—"if we could just get to *there*"—I can promise you one thing: once you get there, it still won't be enough. So what happened?

What happened is this: it was never about having enough to begin with. Enough was never the goal. Enough is a lie you tell yourself. The real goal was, is, and always will be having *more*. More is the goal. And the reason *more* is so important to you is because you've subconsciously bought into the three pillars of materialism: all you need to be satisfied, secure, and significant is a little bit more.

If I have more, you think, *I'll finally be able buy a few things I want right now but can't afford. And these things will make me more satisfied.*

That line of thought leads to worrying.

If I have more, I can finally stop worrying. I won't have to be afraid about this or that happening, this or that crisis, this or that major, unexpected expense. I won't have to worry about retirement or my kids' college tuition. My family will be safe and secure.

And then you think about significance.

If I have more, I will finally have legitimized myself, not only in my own eyes but in everyone else's eyes too. In the eyes of my parents, in the eyes of my peers, in the eyes of my relatives, and my colleagues, and my competitors, and my classmates from college and high school, and in the eyes of my old girlfriends or boyfriends. No one will be able to look down on me any longer because now I've got more than they do, and how can you argue with that?

Do you see it? These are the things that you believe, and you don't even realize you believe them because the first thing materialism does is blind you to the fact that you're materialistic.

YOUR NEXT COUNTERARGUMENT might go along these lines: "Let's say you're right. Let's say that I *am* a devout materialist, that I do want more. If that's true, why is it a problem? These ideas don't sound so terrible or so ridiculous. What's so bad about these beliefs anyway?"

Here's what's so bad about the three tenets of materialism: they all happen to be lies. They are all fundamentally untrue. And if you base your life on lies, you will always be unfulfilled and never know why.

Let's look at these three beliefs one at a time to see how false they really are.

First—the idea that more money will make you happy because you'll be able to buy houses and cars and clothes and furniture and trips and experiences and whatever else you can't currently afford. Do you know how long those things satisfy? You do know, because there are things you currently own that were once objects of desire. You once thought they would make you happy. And they did—at first. But after a while, it wears off. How excited are your kids about last year's Christmas presents? Having more *does* increase happiness—for a week or maybe a month or perhaps even a year. But rarely longer.

Second—the idea that money will make you safe and secure, that if you had more you wouldn't have to worry. But what, in the end, can money really do? Not to be morbid, but think about it: money can't protect you from a car accident or from cancer. Money can't protect your kids and can't control the decisions they make or what other people do to them. Money can't protect your marriage or keep you from getting a divorce or keep your family together. In other words, when it comes to safety and security, money can't do anything that really matters. You might say, "Yes, but if none of those things happen, I'll have enough to live comfortably in retirement." If that's your definition of security, you need to take another look.

Third—the idea that money can give you status and significance in the eyes of others and in your own eyes. There's a twofold problem with this:

1. When you get more, many people won't even notice.
2. Those who do notice won't necessarily respect you for it. They'll usually find a way to judge you instead. Say you earned your money the hard way, through smarts and hard work. Do you think other people will see it that way? More likely, other people will just think you got lucky.

More money cannot give you satisfaction, security, or significance. In fact, what it actually gives you—the real yield of materialism and the true curse of materialism—is the exact opposite of those three things.

Materialism itself keeps you constantly dissatisfied. The belief that additional possessions can increase your happiness is the very thing that robs you of happiness.

Materialism itself makes you feel insecure. The idea that security can somehow be attained, that safety is within reach, is the very thing that cultivates a strong sense of insecurity.

Materialism itself leads to a sense of insignificance. The thought that significance can be found by bettering ourselves in comparison with others or by climbing higher on the ladder of success is the very thing that causes us to feel insignificant.

DO YOU SEE how insidious materialism is? How dark this curse is?

The belief that money can solve your problems is itself the source of those very problems to begin with, which is why materialism is such a powerfully closed system. Not only does it hide itself, but it also makes itself indispensable. First, it creates problems, and then it promises to solve the problems it just created. As long as you buy into it, the problems won't go away. You will feel the need for solutions, which means you keep buying into the system, which means you keep feeding the problems.

It's a vicious circle if there ever was one.

You may have known, somewhere in the back of your mind, that more money wasn't truly the answer to all your problems. But what you may not have known, what may not have even occurred to you, is that the quest for more money is actually the *cause* of all your problems.

You've heard that the Bible says, "The love of money is a root of all kinds of evil" (1 Tim. 6:10). You thought that was a religious cliché. You didn't realize it was a penetrating diagnosis of your most fundamental spiritual and psychological problem.

It's a trap you've fallen into unwittingly, and now you can't get out of it. Because someone wants to keep you there.

11

Materialism Is a Religion

aterialism isn't an atheistic religion. At its center is a very real, very particular god. Jesus talks about this in the Sermon on the Mount:

> No one can serve two masters. Either you will hate the one and love the other, or you will be devoted to the one and despise the other. You cannot serve both God and money. (Matt. 6:24)

Notice what Jesus is doing here. He's personifying money. He isn't talking about it as an object. He's talking about money as a person, a being.

If you look at this passage in the King James Version, you'll see that it says, "You cannot serve both God and mammon." *Mammon* is the more literal translation of the Greek word used here. Mammon was a proper name—the name of a pagan god of wealth.

So Jesus isn't talking about God versus a thing; he's talking about the one true God versus another god. He is describing two potential masters, two deities, either of which a human being can serve, love, and worship. The first potential master is God, and the second potential master is this other deity named Mammon—or money. Money could be written here with a capital *M*, because in this case it's a name.

Jesus says you have to choose which god you want to worship because these two gods are enemies. They're both very demanding. Whichever one you choose will consume all your love and devotion to the point that you will inevitably—there's no way around it—hate and despise the other by comparison. So if you choose the god Mammon, you'll end up despising the one true God. But if you chose the one true God, you'll end up despising Mammon.

Two things have always surprised me about the way Jesus sets this up. The first is that it's totally binary. There's no such thing as having one foot in both camps. There's no spectrum. You can't be 70 percent for one deity and 30 percent for the other. It is all or none, one or the other, which tells us a lot about what these two particular deities are like. They are so demanding—so all encompassing—that whether you realize it, you'll be entirely devoted to one or the other. It can't be both.

The second surprising thing is that Jesus doesn't say it's God versus the world or God versus sin or God versus Satan or God versus evil or God versus pleasure. No. It's God versus *money*. Jesus could have chosen anything. Why money?

The likeliest explanation is that in Jesus's day, just as in our day, money was the god that gave the one true God the stiffest competition.

For much of the Old Testament, the main rival to the one true God was a god named Baal. All through Israel's history, the prophets gave sermons like, "No one can serve two masters. Either you will hate the one and love the other, or you will be devoted to the one and despise the other. You cannot serve both God and Baal."[1] Yet the people continued to try to serve both gods simultaneously.

Baal eventually faded—the people finally figured out that he wasn't real—but the practice of trying to worship two gods at the same time persisted. Mammon took Baal's place as the most popular rival to the one true God. And this is still true today. Money isn't just *one* of the false gods that vie for our worship. It is, far and away, the one true God's fiercest competitor.

NOW THAT WE HAVE a basic understanding of how this either/or dynamic works, I want to ask you two questions. First, which of the two gods do you worship? Second, which of the two gods do you therefore hate?

You are the only one who knows. No one can tell from the outside, and appearances can be deceiving. Plenty of poorer saints secretly worship money. Likewise, plenty of successful businesspeople worship God. Only you can say, but to help you figure it out, let me give you a self-diagnostic test:

When you think about something constantly,
When you give all your time and energy in pursuit of
   something,

When you trust in something to take care of you,
When you look to something for safety and security,
When you find in something your sense of identity and
   significance,
When you equate something with happiness,
That *something* is the god you worship.

You might respond, "Are you trying to suggest I worship money?" No. Why do you ask? Is money what came to mind just now? I was simply describing what worship looks like. If that description of worship made you think of money, that's coming from you, not me.

WE COULD GO BACK AND FORTH about this all day, but we don't have to because there's one definitive way to figure out which of the two gods you worship. It's a fool-proof litmus test. Paul describes it in 2 Corinthians 8:7–8: "But since you excel in everything—in faith, in speech, in knowledge, in complete earnestness and in the love we have kindled in you—see that you also excel in this grace of giving. I am not commanding you, but I want to test the sincerity of your love."

In essence, Paul says to the church at Corinth, "I see you have some of the signs of people who love God. You've got faith, you've got speech, and you've got knowledge. You *seem* to be very earnest. It *appears* that you really love and worship God. But, of course, there's one way we can know for sure. It's this issue of whether you give him your money." A lot of people *say* they love and worship God, but there is only one surefire test of the sincerity of that love.

You might be offended by that statement. You might object, "Are you really suggesting that this is the only way to prove I love God? That's ridiculous. What about praying? What about reading the Bible? What about serving others? What about being involved at church and volunteering and giving my time and my abilities? There are all sorts of ways to give to God. It's not all about money."

But it is all about money right now. That's what we're talking about. We're talking about a showdown between two rival deities: God on the one hand and money on the other. Money is the only competing god in question at the moment.

So if you say to the one true God, "I will give you *anything*, I will give you *everything*, except my money," don't you think that reveals quite clearly who the real winner is?

ONE OF THE REASONS I LOVE the annual offering season at our church is because it feels like the Super Bowl. It's the time when the two biggest heavyweights—the two strongest deities in our culture—go head-to-head to find out who's gonna be No. 1. It reminds me of the contest Elijah set up between Baal and Yahweh on Mount Carmel: "Who's going to be God in this land?" (1 Kings 18). It reminds me of when Joshua called for a vote: "Choose this day whom you will serve" (Josh. 24:15).

That's what our annual offering is. It's voting time. It's the time we meet as a family every year and say, "OK. It's that time again. Who's going to be God in this church? Which god will we worship? There are two candidates seeking the job. On this side, we have the God of Abraham, Isaac, and Jacob—he would like to be worshiped in this church. Over here, we have Mammon. He wants the same position. Who will it be this year?"

And then we vote. "Who's for God? Who's for Mammon?" We don't vote by a show of hands or with a ballot. That would mean nothing. Instead, we vote with our wallets.

When the gifts are tallied, the reason I rejoice isn't because the offering was a "success." Rather, I rejoice because it means that God *won*. It means that for at least one more year, our church will be a church in which the one true God is worshiped. The votes are in, and God is victorious.

But every year, I know there are people in our church who choose to side with Mammon instead. It's heartbreaking, not because it affects the total but because I know that it means those individuals won't grow spiritually in the year ahead.

The number one thing keeping most Christians from experiencing a deeper relationship with the God of the Bible is that they already have another god. And any effort toward spiritual growth is largely a waste of time until that issue is dealt with.

Say you have a married friend who is having an ongoing affair. He might say, "You know, I'd really like to get closer to my wife. I'd like to strengthen my marriage. What can I do? Maybe we should go on more dates, spend more time together, talk more."

You respond, "You should start by ending that affair."

To which he replies, "What? The affair? Oh, no, you don't understand—that's unrelated. That's completely separate.

I'm talking about my *wife*. I want to get closer to her. What does the affair have to do with it?"

This is how it is for many Christians when it comes to growing closer to God. They say, "I want to get closer to God. I'm going to try some things. I'll pray more, join a small group, read the Bible, and go to church more often."

But for many of you, my response to those intentions would be to say, "Don't waste your time." Because your heart already belongs to someone else.

12

Giving Is the Only Way Out

hy does giving break the spell of materialism like nothing else can? The answer is straightforward. Materialism says *more* is the answer. When you give, you're making a deliberate decision to have *less*, at least in the short run. So giving, on a fundamental and philosophical level, is as antimaterialistic as you can get.

It's worth pausing here to point out that giving is the only solution that works. All sorts of other ideas and methods for dealing with materialism will suggest themselves to you, but none of them actually address the problem.

For example, merely getting rid of some things won't work. Nor will making a resolution to spend less. It won't help to purge or downsize or sell your second home. None of these actions is antimaterialistic at their core, because none of these things make your bottom line go down. If you downsize or sell your second home, you keep the money.

When you stop splurging, you still have the money to spend on something else.

And you will—eventually. If you stop spending money on this over here, you will start spending it on that over there. When you get rid of stuff, you get new stuff. While decluttering, spending less, saving more, and selling things might all be good ideas for some reason unrelated to materialism, don't expect them to have any effect on the grip of materialism itself.

Likewise, it won't help to drop out of the rat race and take a lower-paying job. That could be part of the answer for a small percentage of people but not most. For most people, again, this won't address the real problem. If you take a lower-paying job, unless the work itself is inherently more satisfying, you're just going to be bitter, asking yourself, What's the point of making so much less than I could be making? It's not the number of dollars in the bank that's the problem; it's the fact that you *want* the number to be higher. You may have less, but you'd still *want* more. It's also why a middle- or lower-class person isn't necessarily less materialistic than a wealthy person. Their desire for more can be just as strong, if not stronger, which means that their need to give is just as urgent as it is for the wealthy.

NO MATTER HOW MUCH MONEY YOU HAVE, giving is the only action that directly moves against the materialistic mindset. It's not just one of several potential approaches. It's *the* key that unlocks the cage.

And if it's going to work, you need to not only give but also give an uncomfortable amount. We talked earlier about how giving an uncomfortable amount was necessary to grow your faith; otherwise, it's not enough to make a difference.

The same principle holds true when it comes to breaking free from materialism. If your giving doesn't hurt, then your attachment to Mammon is unaffected. The discomfort of your giving is the only proof that you're accomplishing something.

You may have seen the T-shirt that reads, "Sweat is fat crying." The brilliance of the slogan is that it personifies fat and makes you think of it as a living thing that wants to survive. Once you start sweating—and only then—does your fat start protesting, "No, don't kill me! Don't get rid of me!" Your fat doesn't care at all if you engage in *moderate* exercise because that doesn't threaten it. It only starts to cry, it only starts to whither and die, when you turn up the heat.

It's the same with giving. Only at the point that your giving makes you wince do you start to actually address the problem. Only then are you finally on the path to freedom. Mammon is fine with you giving a little bit. It doesn't mind when you chip in or support a good cause. It has no problem at all with moderate, charitable giving. In fact, Mammon is a *fan* of charitable giving, because people who give moderately and charitably can convince themselves that they aren't materialistic after all and are thus much *less* likely to attack the real challenge.

But if you give until it hurts, then you begin to choke materialism itself. As materialism suffocates, you start to breathe easier. This is why I tell the people at our church that they should actually be giving *violently*, giving with the express intent to kill materialism. It's a fight for your life. If you don't kill it, it's going to kill you. Not until you start suffocating and choking materialism will you see that it has been suffocating and choking you all along.

The reason no one thinks they worship money is because money itself, the god we've made of it, has a vested interest in concealing that fact. Money wants to make us think that *it* serves *us*. But actually, *we* serve *it*. Money is not a manly, straightforward, up-front sort of god. It doesn't come and openly ask us for our worship as the real God does. Rather, money says, "I'll help you. I'll be your servant. I'll get you what you want." But before you know it, the tables are turned and it's the other way around. Instead of it working for you, you're working for it. Instead of you owning it, it owns you. You were tricked. And now it has sunk its claws so deep into you that you're trapped.

The sociologist Max Weber once observed that the Puritans thought they could wear a concern for money and material goods like a light cloak on their shoulders, which could be thrown aside at any moment. But then Weber devastatingly commented, "But fate decreed that the cloak should become an iron cage."[1] It wasn't just fate, of course. This trick, the cloak turning into a cage, was planned all along. Edmund Burke, the English statesman, said, "We are bought by the enemy with the treasure in our own coffers."[2]

IF GIVING FEELS LIKE the last thing you want to do, that proves you need to do it all the more. That feeling—"No, I don't want to give; I'm afraid I won't have enough left"—is money tightening its fingers around your neck and saying, "Don't desert me. I'm the god you should worship. I'll take care of you. I won't let you down."

If you're happy thus far with the god you've chosen, there's no reason to make a change. If money has delivered on its promises and kept its word—if it has given you peace and fulfillment, reduced your stress, and increased your joy—then my advice would be to stick with money. Be true to your god. There's no reason to jump ship now if everything is working out. If you're already satisfied, why make a change?

On the other hand, if the honeymoon has ended, and you've discovered that money can be a mean and nasty god—a cruel, domineering slave driver who works you to the bone and overpromises but underdelivers—then my question is, Why on earth would you listen to money any longer? Why would you listen again to money's empty promises? It has lied to you before, and it is lying to you again. To listen would be nothing short of insanity.

The truth is, you're under its spell. You're like an addict who has lost all sense of self-awareness. The only way out—the only way to break the spell and slay the beast and loose the chains and get your life back—is to give. When you give, you take a spear and drive it into Mammon's heart. You take this idol and throw it into the sea, saying,

"I will no longer worship you."

"I will no longer depend on you."

"I will no longer let you ruin my life."

I'D LIKE TO YIELD the rest of this chapter to a man from our church, so he can tell you how this played out in his own life. Enter Tim.

I wouldn't say that I grew up in an environment overly focused on wealth accumulation. But after college as I was entering the workforce, the idea of making increasing amounts of money over time was certainly one of my primary goals. It also became one of the main ways I defined success and, therefore, a fundamental part of my sense of self-worth.

To me, making *enough* money came down to two things. One was security for the future: having enough to send kids to college and enough to retire. But a second element also entered in, the whole concept of *trading up*: the accumulation of more and better stuff. I never considered myself overly materialistic. But I did fall into the trap of thinking that as a person gets better jobs and starts making more money, they should naturally start thinking about getting a nicer car or a bigger house, even if they don't technically need it.

This felt very normal for a time, and I didn't see anything unhealthy about it. But then I recognized that this belief was becoming a bit weightier in my thinking, and I was becoming a bit more dysfunctional in relation to it. The part I disliked most was that it became increasingly based on comparing myself to others. I would look at other people and think, *I have the same kind of job as them and probably earn a similar amount, but they just moved to a bigger house in a nicer neighborhood and have a nicer car. Maybe we should move into a bigger house in a nicer neighborhood*—even though we were very happy in the house we were in.

Around this time, my company moved me from North Carolina to New York City. That's when this view of financial success started to fall apart. Most people who move to New York realize before very long that they can't keep up.

There is virtually no ceiling on incomes; there are people who make astronomical amounts that are not just a certain percentage more than you but many levels higher than you. This meant that evaluating success by my old standards, some relative accumulation of material possessions, was always going to be a losing battle.

It was while I was internally debating this and trying to recalibrate what success means to me that I first heard the messages on giving at our church. The sermons presented many different reasons for why we should give. All the reasons made sense, but only one of them really resonated with me emotionally: you should give for the sole reason of breaking the hold that money has on you. For the first time, I was introduced to the idea that though we may feel as though we're controlling our money, in reality our money is controlling us. This rang true to me.

Ryan said the only way to break the grip of money was to give it away. He went as far as saying: "If you decide not to give your money away to a church or a charity, then burn it. Just get rid of it so it can't control you. That would be healthier spiritually than saving and storing it." The point was that our main motivation for giving doesn't need to be altruism. It's not really about how the money ultimately gets used or what it accomplishes. It's more about preserving our own sanity and personally breaking free from its hold on us.

I will admit that, at first, burning my money sounded ridiculous. I wasn't going to do that. Even the idea of giving away a large amount of money and not really caring how it was used seemed strange.

But because the part about the grip of money rang so true for me, my wife and I decided to give it a try. We said,

"We're going to take the plunge, give more than what feels comfortable, and see what happens."

Though our lives didn't change overnight, there's no question that it worked. There was this change—slow at first, and then building—this growing feeling that we weren't running the same race anymore because we had chosen to drop out. Because we were not chasing a standard of financial success that somehow always felt out of reach, we both felt a sense of financial freedom we had not felt before.

We've continued to participate in aggressive, uncomfortable giving for the past five years, and the effect has only become more pronounced. We continue to think differently about the role of money in our lives and how we define success. Over time, this practice has given us the feeling that we're more in control of our finances rather than our finances controlling us.

I've always wanted to be able to give out of some deep philanthropic or spiritual place. But the truth is, as much as I've tried to drum up those motives, they are not there. They haven't made me want to give enough or consistently enough. The idea of breaking the hold of money is what has worked for me. As much as I wish I could say that I'm giving out of pure benevolence, if I'm being honest, it has only been this more selfish motivation (peace of mind) that's driven me to become more generous.

Reward #3

Financial Provision

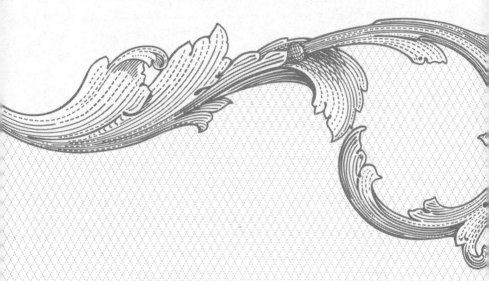

13

God Promises to Provide

he main reason people don't give is also the most obvious: they feel they can't afford to. Many people say something along these lines: "One day, I hope to have more, and then of course I'll be more generous. But right now happens to be a bad time. It's been a tough year." Becoming more generous is something a lot of people would really like to do—someday.

What I've also discovered is that this mindset is completely unaffected by how much money a person actually makes. Let's say you make X. You think to yourself, "If I just made Y, then I could give a lot." The problem with that is, I could show you a person who already makes Y, and they don't give much either because their expenses have increased in proportion to their income.

So everybody thinks, *If I had enough, then I would give.* But nobody, no matter how much they have, feels like they have enough.

As is the case in so many areas, Jesus takes the conventional wisdom and turns it directly on its head. It's not that if you had enough you would give. It's that only once you start to give will you ever have enough. As it turns out, "giving" and "having enough" do go together after all. We were right about that much. But the causal link between them runs in exactly the opposite direction than we thought.

IN THE PREVIOUS PART OF THIS BOOK, we looked at Jesus's teaching about God versus Mammon in the Sermon on the Mount. In this chapter, we'll look at the same verse but now in a fuller context.

> No one can serve two masters. Either you will hate the one and love the other, or you will be devoted to the one and despise the other. You cannot serve both God and money.
>
> Therefore, I tell you, do not worry about your life, what you will eat or drink; . . . what you will wear. . . . Look at the birds of the air. . . .
>
> See how the flowers of the field grow. . . . If that is how God clothes the grass of the field, which is here today and tomorrow is thrown into the fire, will he not much more clothe you—you of little faith? So do not worry, saying, "What shall we eat?" or "What shall we drink?" or "What shall we wear?" For the pagans run after all these things, and your heavenly Father knows that you need them. But seek first his kingdom . . . and all these things will be given to you as well. (Matt. 6:24–33)

This is one of the most well-known passages in all of Scripture, but it's also one of the most misunderstood. What is Jesus really talking about here?

Let's start by acknowledging the part we can all agree on: he's telling us not to worry about our physical needs. There's little confusion about that. But *why* does he want us not to worry, and how does he expect us to stop?

If you read the passage literally, what Jesus seems to be saying is to just trust God to pay our bills. Because he will. He'll take care of us just like he takes care of the birds of the air and the flowers of the field. Yet most of us quickly conclude that he couldn't possibly be saying that. We dismiss the literal interpretation out of hand because it's so difficult for us to imagine how it would happen. Do clothes and food just show up on our doorstep? Does he find an apartment for us and pay the rent? Does God send us checks in the mail? Or does he skip that step and send checks directly to the people we owe?

Because it all seems so ridiculous, we decide this must not be what the passage means. So we try to find some other interpretation that's easier to defend. "Perhaps Jesus is simply talking about a mindset here," we reason. "He must mean that I'm supposed to go about my business normally, but in the midst of it, I should try really hard not to worry—that I should do all the same things I usually do, while reminding myself that God loves me and is taking care of me. That's what it is."

But that's *not* what it is. This second, less-literal interpretation—the idea that Jesus is simply talking about a state of mind—is wrong. Rather, the first interpretation, the literal, ridiculous-sounding one—about God sending you checks in the mail and making money show up in your account and arranging for your bills to be paid—is correct. That is what Jesus is talking about here. He's saying not to worry about your financial needs, because God will literally, actually, take care of them for you.

You might say, "But that's never happened for me." And I'd reply, "I bet you're right—I bet it has never happened for you." You might have thought I would say, "I'm sure it's happened for you, you just didn't realize it; you just weren't paying attention." But that's not my view. That's a cop-out. My guess is that God probably hasn't ever provided for your needs in this sort of way, and I bet I know why.

MANY OF THE PROMISES OF THE BIBLE have an interesting feature. They aren't *promises* at all, at least not in the traditional sense. Instead of being one-way, unilateral proclamations, they are two-way, bilateral contracts. They are covenants in which each side has a part to play: God and us. As we talked about in chapter 8, they are if-then statements: "If you do that, then I will do this." There is some confusion on this point, because the love of God is 100 percent unconditional, sheer grace. But many of the specific benefits God promises are totally dependent on our actions.

In this passage in the Sermon on the Mount, what is the if-then statement? Where does Jesus describe our end of the deal? It's easy to miss, because it's a little bit hidden and it comes in the last line. Jesus says: "Seek first [God's] kingdom . . . and all these things will be given to [us] as well."

There it is—that's our part. *If* we seek first his kingdom, *then* God will take care of our needs. Our part is to seek the kingdom of God above all else. God's part, if and only if we do our part, is to give us everything we need, to make sure that "all these things will be given to [us] as well."

That, of course, leads to another question: What does it mean to "seek first his kingdom"? Now we've come to another one of the reasons this passage is so commonly misunderstood. People think of seeking God's kingdom first as this very vague, very big spiritual concept. They translate it in their minds as *being a super Christian* or *leaving your job to become a missionary.*

But that's not what "seek first his kingdom" means, at least not in this passage. It's not a vague standard of super-spirituality. Quite the opposite, actually. In this passage, seeking first the kingdom of God can be boiled down to one very tangible, very practical, very specific thing, and we can figure out what that thing is by looking at the context of the passage as a whole.

LET'S STEP BACK for a moment to ask a preliminary question: What is this passage about? It's usually thought of as being a passage about worry, and in one sense it is. But on a deeper level, it's about something else. Think back to how the passage begins: "No one can serve two masters. Either you will hate the one and love the other, or you will be devoted to the one and despise the other. You cannot serve both God and money."

That's the intro. What's the conclusion? In Luke 12:22–33, Jesus closes this passage by saying, "Do not be afraid. . . . Sell your possessions and give to the poor."

So you see, Jesus begins by talking about money. He ends by talking about money. And in the middle, he talks about the types of material needs that require money. Putting all that together, this famous "worry" passage isn't about worrying after all. It is about the one specific subject we're most prone to worry about: money.

When Jesus says to seek first the kingdom of God, that might include a number of material things, but the one thing it certainly includes, the one thing he has to be talking about, is money. What does it mean to seek first the kingdom of God? It means to give your money first to God's kingdom, before you meet your own physical needs. *Seek first his kingdom*, then comes the promise: *if* you do that, *then* God himself will provide for you financially.

ONCE ALL OF THAT IS UNDERSTOOD, many people respond generally along these lines: "No wonder I've never experienced this. I've never done that, . . . and I'm never going to do that. That's irresponsible. That's impossible." Once people see the deal that's actually being offered, they don't want it anymore. "I have to do what? You've gotta be kidding."

But at least now you know what is being offered. And at least now you know why you still worry, why you have not witnessed God providing for you in dramatic fashion. You simply haven't held up your end of the bargain.

Many people think, *I know that God is going to take care of my needs. I know that's true—I believe it—but I just have a hard time feeling it.*

But maybe it's *not* true—for you. God promised to take care of your needs *if* you give your money to him first, before anything else. He never promised to take care of you while you were going around trying to take care of yourself.

If you're keeping your money for yourself and saying, "I just have a hard time believing that God is going to take care of this stuff," he's not. Nobody ever said he was going to, not as long as you're on the job. You misunderstood. You're on your own, and all your worry is well justified. You should be worried. Somebody better worry, because it's you against the world.

14

Over and Over Again

n the last chapter, we looked at God's promise to materially provide for those who give their money to him. But this teaching isn't limited to a single passage. In this chapter, we're going to look at six other passages that say the same thing. For those of you who aren't convinced that this idea is truly biblical, my goal is to *inundate* you with evidence. (If, on the other hand, you're already convinced that this is how it works, you can skip ahead to chapter 15.)

THE FIRST PASSAGE, also the most famous and most explicit, that teaches about God's material provision in response to giving is Malachi 3:10–12. God says:

"Bring the whole tithe into the storehouse, that there may be food in my house. Test me in this," says the LORD Almighty, "and see if I will not throw open the floodgates of heaven and pour out so much blessing that there will not be room enough to store it. I will prevent pests from devouring your crops, and the vines in your fields will not drop their fruit before it is ripe," says the LORD Almighty. "Then all the nations will call you blessed, for yours will be a delightful land," says the LORD Almighty.

In regard to this passage, I've found that there are two groups of people. The first is those who have tried it and know that it works. The second is those who haven't tried it and, therefore, try to explain this passage out of the Bible, arguing that it no longer applies to us.

People have said to me, "That's just a one-off passage." But it's not. Because almost every time the tithe is mentioned in the Bible, what God says is, "Tithe, so I can bless you."

Likewise, people have said to me, "That's just an Old Testament promise made specifically to Israel." So should we dismiss it as not applying to us? No. God makes hundreds of promises to Israel in the Old Testament. It's true that many of them apply to only Israel in that particular time and place. Many others, however, should legitimately be interpreted as applying to all believers in all times and places. Scripture says that the church should be thought of as a continuation of Israel. The church, like Israel, is God's "chosen people."

The question is, then, "How do we know which promises apply to us?" There's a very simple test: if the promise is repeated in the New Testament, it's fair to claim the promise from the Old Testament passage as well. For example, when you ask people what their favorite Bible verse is, many will quote Jeremiah 29:11: "'For I know the plans I have for you,' declares the LORD, 'plans to prosper you and not to harm you, plans to give you hope and a future.'" In the context of the book of Jeremiah, this is clearly a promise to a specific group of Jews in a specific time and place. Are Christian believers today misguided when they read this promise as applying to them? Absolutely not, because the same promise is repeated in various ways all through the New Testament. In other words, it still holds true, so quote it with confidence.

The same goes for Malachi 3. Because this same promise is repeated in the New Testament, as we'll see in this chapter, the Old Testament promise can be claimed by believers today as well.

THE SECOND PASSAGE is Philippians 4:15–19. Paul writes:

> As you know, you Philippians were the only ones who gave me financial help when I first brought you the Good News. . . . I don't say this because I want a gift from you. Rather, I want you to receive a reward for your kindness.
>
> At the moment I have all I need—and more! I am generously supplied with the gifts you sent me. . . . They are a sweet-smelling sacrifice that is acceptable and pleasing to God. And this same God who takes care of me will supply all your needs from his glorious riches. (NLT)

Again here, as with the passage in Matthew 6 from the Sermon on the Mount that we looked at in the previous chapter, we have a case of a famous verse that's often been taken out of context. Verse 19—"God . . . will supply all your needs from his glorious riches"—is usually quoted as a universal assurance to all Christians everywhere. But just as with Matthew 6, this promise has a condition. Paul makes this assertion only *in light of* the generous giving to the church's work, Paul's work, that has been undertaken by the Philippians.

The idea that God will supply all your needs from his riches only applies if you've given to his work. If you've held up your end of the deal—and only if you've held up your end of the deal—then it's a promise. God will give back to you and make sure you have enough.

Verse 17 is remarkable. The New International Version translates it this way: "Not that I desire your gifts; what I desire is that more be credited to your account." Paul is saying that the greatest benefit of giving always goes to the givers themselves, the profit that is credited to the account of every individual who gives. This account should be thought of primarily in terms of eternity—treasure in heaven, which we'll look at in a later part of the book. But given the rest of the scriptural testimony, it's fair to read this passage as referring to earthly blessing as well.

THE THIRD PASSAGE is 2 Corinthians 9:6–11. Paul says:

> Remember this—a farmer who plants only a few seeds will get a small crop. But the one who plants generously will get a generous crop. . . . And God will generously provide all you need. Then you will always have everything you need and plenty left over to share with others. . . .

He will provide and increase your resources and then pro-
duce a great harvest of generosity in you.

Yes, you will be enriched in every way so that you can
always be generous. (NLT)

While the first two passages teach that the person who
gives will always have enough—always have their basic needs
met—this third passage suggests that God will make sure
the person who gives has *more* than enough.

Verse 6 talks about a farmer sowing and reaping. The
amount of grain that is harvested is *in proportion* to the
amount of seed that was sown. But critically, the total *volume* of grain will always be much greater than the volume of
seed. That's the nature of sowing and reaping—you always
get back more than you put in. It multiplies. And Paul says
that's exactly how it works with giving.

So why does God provide so generously to those who give?
Paul repeats the same answer three times in this passage:

God is able to give you more than you need, so that you
will always have all you need for yourselves and more than
enough for every good cause. (v. 8 GNT)

He will provide and increase your resources and then pro-
duce a great harvest of generosity in you. (v. 10 NLT)

You will be enriched in every way so that you can be generous on every occasion. (v. 11)

We'll talk more about this principle in the next chapter, but
I'll briefly introduce it here. The reason God gives back to those

who give to him is so that those same people can give even more the next time around. God is not stupid. He sees which people put resources where he wants them to go, and then he directs more resources to those people with the expectation that they will continue to give as they have in the past. When God blesses you in response to your giving, it's not that he's only giving *to* you but that he's also giving *through* you. He doesn't bless us financially so that we can raise our standard of living, but rather so we can raise our standard of giving.

THE FOURTH PASSAGE is Luke 6:38, which I'll mention only in passing. Jesus says:

> Give, and you will receive. Your gift will return to you in full—pressed down, shaken together to make room for more, running over, and poured into your lap. The amount you give will determine the amount you get back. (NLT)

At first, this appears to be a very direct and explicit example of the promise to provide for those who give. But it's important to note that this statement comes in the context of Jesus discussing interpersonal relationships: he's talking primarily about giving to and receiving from other people, not God.

However, given the preceding passages, it seems fair to expand the interpretation and see this passage too as applying to giving and receiving from God. At the very least, it's still another example of what appears, from the biblical point of view, to be a universal law: you always get back more than you put in.

THE FIFTH PASSAGE is 1 Kings 17:8–15, the story of Elijah and the widow.

> Then the LORD said to Elijah, "Go and live in the village of Zarephath. . . . I have instructed a widow there to feed you." . . .
>
> As he arrived at the gates of the village, he saw a widow gathering sticks, and he asked her, . . . "Bring me a bite of bread. . . ."
>
> But she said, "I swear by the LORD your God that I don't have a single piece of bread in the house. And I have only a handful of flour left in the jar and a little cooking oil in the bottom of the jug. I was just gathering a few sticks to cook this last meal, and then my son and I will die."
>
> But Elijah said to her, "Don't be afraid! Go ahead and do just what you've said, but make a little bread for me first. Then use what's left to prepare a meal for yourself and your son. For this is what the LORD, the God of Israel, says: There will always be flour and olive oil left in your containers until the time when the LORD sends rain and the crops grow again!"
>
> So she did as Elijah said, and she and Elijah and her family continued to eat for many days. There was always enough flour and olive oil left in the containers, just as the LORD had promised through Elijah. (NLT)

The principle of how giving and receiving work might seem to be a one-time event in the case of this widow, but the general principle is stated clearly elsewhere. So it's legitimate to take this story as an example of how it works for all of us, not just for this woman.

The woman supported God's prophet first, before taking care of herself and her own son. She sought first God's kingdom—not worrying about what she herself would eat. And "all these things" were given to her—God provided for her in response to her sacrificial giving.

THE SIXTH AND FINAL PASSAGE is one we looked at earlier, but it's worth looking at it again in greater depth. It's Jacob's vow in Genesis 28:20–22 to give God a tenth of all God gave him.

> Then Jacob made a vow, saying, "If God will be with me and will watch over me on this journey I am taking and will give me food to eat and clothes to wear so that I return safely to my father's household, then the LORD will be my God . . . , and of all that you give me I will give you a tenth."

This is another great example of something we've seen in this book thus far. In contrast to the mature, noble, and selfless posture that many people try to strike today, what's seen time and time again in Scripture is that the heroes of the faith are not embarrassed about their true motives. They want God on their side. They want God helping them in their business affairs. They want God fighting their battles.

Jacob makes a vow—in other words, a pledge—to God. It's a pledge about money; he promises to give God a tenth. But why is Jacob pledging to give God a tenth? He tells us plainly: he wants God to watch over his journey and give him food to eat and clothes to wear. He says, "If God will be with me." His giving is *conditioned* on the assumption that God will provide in response.

Jacob's reference to food and clothing should remind us of something we've read. What Jacob is talking about in Genesis 28 is what Jesus is talking about in Matthew 6. Jesus says that if we give God our money, he'll provide food and clothes for us. Jacob says he is giving God his money specifically because he wants God to provide food and clothes for him. He's saying, in effect, "I don't want to have to worry. I want things to go well. I'm going to give you a piece of my pie so that you'll get involved in my business affairs."

This is exactly what giving does. Giving makes God a business partner. You're cutting God in. And, to state the obvious, that's the best business decision you're ever going to make.

In any business, why does anyone bring in a partner? Why would you let them have a slice of your pie? If you give *them* a slice, your slice will be smaller. Why would you do that? Simply because you like the person and want someone to go to lunch with?

No. The reason you bring in a partner is because it's not a zero-sum game. Yes, your percentage of the pie gets smaller. But since the pie gets bigger, your bottom line goes up.

Can't you see that it's the same with God? Can't you see that 90 percent or 80 percent or 70 percent of your income with God is going to be so much greater than 100 percent of your income without him? The larger a percentage of your "business" you give to him, the more he can grow your business.

TO SUM UP, this promise of provision is repeated all through the Bible. It's in the Old Testament as well as the New. It's in the Law and also the Prophets. It's in the teachings of Jesus and the writings of Paul. It's everywhere.

And not only is it repeated over and over again in Scripture, it has also been repeated over and over again in people's experiences today. Over the last decade, we have paraded person after person across the stage of our church with one remarkable story after another. The details of their stories are different, but the basic story line is always the same: "I gave an amount that felt incredibly risky to me, more than I ever thought I could. And then God provided for me financially in this bizarre, unexpected way that I never saw coming, from somewhere that wasn't even on my radar."

Not only does God give back to those who give to him, but he gives back more to those who give more. The bolder you are in your giving, the more generous God is in response. You cannot outgive God.

15

Why It Works This Way

Despite the solid scriptural witness, I've discovered that many Bible-believing Christians still struggle to believe that God will materially provide in response to our giving. In this chapter, I want to offer two more supporting arguments. First, I'll offer an argument based on logic: why it absolutely must work this way as a matter of necessity. Second, I'll offer an argument that is more relational and aesthetic: why it's so good and beautiful that it works this way.

FIRST, THE LOGICAL ARGUMENT. In the field of logic, one accepted way of demonstrating the necessity of an idea is to show that the opposite of that idea is flawed. It's called a *reductio ad absurdum*, which is Latin for "reduced to absurdity." (This is the only thing I remember from my philosophy major.) This is the form of argument I want to employ here. If the opposite of an idea doesn't hold up, then the idea itself is true.

Let's assume for a moment the opposite of what the Bible claims—God does *not* provide for those who give their money to him. He wants people to give, but he's not going to give them anything in return. He simply expects them to do it out of obedience and a spirit of sacrifice.

If that were the case, what would happen? It's not too hard to figure out. Everyone who gave to God's work *would eventually run out of money.* This would mean two things.

First, other people would see this and think, *Now I know what not to do.* If children saw their parents do this, they'd think, *Note to self: don't do that.* The concept of being a sacrificial giver would die out in one generation, because people would see that it simply didn't work.

There's also a second—and to me, even more interesting—thing that would happen. Let's assume that despite not receiving anything back in return, the original givers still wanted to give more. The problem is, if they had truly given beyond their means the first time, and God didn't give back, they now wouldn't have anything *left* to give. They gave, and now the money is gone.

As the original givers ran out of money and as potential new givers were dissuaded from giving by seeing this example, what would the result be? The money would eventually dry up, and the work would die out.

Do you see what I'm getting at?

If God wants his work in the world to continue, and the means for enabling that work is people giving to support it, *his only option* is to give back to those who give to him. It's a necessity. In the last chapter I mentioned a point that I said we'd come back to. Here it is. The ultimate reason God gives back to those who give to him is *not* so that those people can get rich. If you want to get rich, there are far easier ways to do it than through giving. Rather, the reason God gives back to those who give to him is so that those same people can give again—and give more. We already saw where Paul says this three times in 2 Corinthians 9. The whole point of God giving back to you is so that you can be even more generous the next time around. You think, *We tried this, we saw God provide for us, so now we're going to try it again and give even more.*

I've seen this happen at our church. In the first part of this book, "Our Story," I shared that the annual giving at our church is thirteen times higher than it was eight years ago, despite attendance being only five times higher. So it's not only that new and more people are giving. Rather, it's also that the same people who gave previously are giving more than they did the year before.

But this raises a question: How is that mathematically possible unless God is enlarging their capacity to give? If God didn't give back to those who give, everyone would be tapped out at some point, and we'd have to set lower and lower goals for our offering each year. Instead, we've had to set larger and larger goals to keep pace with God. The more people give, the more their capacity to give keeps growing. I've seen the incomes of people in our church go through the roof as they keep daring God by giving bigger and bigger amounts.

God is looking for people who are putting resources where he wants them to go. When he finds them, he says, "I'm going to send more resources there, because in the past, they've ended up where I wanted them to end up." In that sense, we're just a pipeline, a conduit. If the diameter of your pipeline keeps expanding, you can eventually get to the point at which you are giving more than you're keeping but still living comfortably off the leftovers. There could be so much water running through your pipe that you could live off just the drips.

You might object, "That's never going to happen for me." How do you know? I know plenty of people who didn't think they could give 10 percent, but now they do and somehow still have enough. I know of others who didn't think they could give 15 percent or 20 percent, but now they do and somehow still have enough. There's absolutely no reason that percentage can't keep climbing. Because as it goes up, God will take notice.

That's the logical argument. Now, let's turn to the relational argument.

SECOND, THE RELATIONAL, AESTHETIC ARGUMENT. The misinterpretation of this book that I am most afraid of, the thing I would be most saddened by, is if you walked away from it thinking that the idea of God giving back to us is the Christian version of karma. That's not at all what I'm saying. I'm not talking about "what goes around comes around" or doing a good deed and being rewarded by the universe. God is not "the universe." God is not a law. God is not a force. Rather, God is a person. And he's not just any person—he's our Father. Remember what

Jesus said: your *Father* knows you need these things.[1] This is the beginning of the beautiful argument for giving to and receiving from God.

As any father knows, providing for our children is one of the ways we express our love for them. Giving them gifts is one of the ways we show that we care. And it runs in the other direction too: our kids enjoy giving gifts to us as an expression of their love for us.

The cycle of giving to God and receiving something back isn't just about "stuff." It's about two people—a father and a child—giving gifts to one another, trying to outdo one another in showing love and affection.

There's a simple reason why God always gives you more in return when you give to him. It's because *he can*. He's *able* to give more to us, just like we're able to give more to our children than they're able to give to us. And God enjoys showing how much he loves us.

It reminds me of a children's book that I used to read to my girls about a daddy rabbit and a little rabbit.[2] The little rabbit spreads out his arms and says, "Dad, I love you this much," and the daddy rabbit spreads out his longer arms and says, "But I love you *this* much." Then the little rabbit stands on his hands and says, "Dad, I love you up to my toes," and the daddy rabbit grabs him by the arms, swings him up into the air, and says, "But I love you up to where your toes are *now*." Then the little rabbit says, "Dad, I love you as high as I can jump." And the daddy rabbit says, "But I love you as high as *I* can jump. Watch."

I used to play a version of this game with my own girls. Our oldest daughter, Reese, learned in school that a human being's heart is about the same size as their fist. She would hold up her clenched fist to me and say, "Dad, I love you this much"—that is, with her whole heart. And then I would put my fist up to hers and say, "But I love you this much." And, of course, my fist was twice the size.

What's interesting about this game is that as much as the child likes it, as much as kids enjoy seeing how much they are loved, the father actually likes it more. The father relishes demonstrating his greater capacity—"I have bigger arms, so I can hold you tighter. I've got a bigger heart, so I can love you better."

This is exactly how the giving game works. This is the dynamic that underpins it. It's this exchange of gifts in which you say, "God, I love you this much." And he responds, "But I love you *this* much."

It's not only about competition but also about imitation. The reason children do all the things they see their father do is because *they want to be like him*. That imitation aspect applies to giving. We've been talking all along as if we give to God first, and then God gives back to us in response. But that's not quite right. When you step back and look at the bigger picture, it's clear that God gave first. God gave you life first. God gave you grace first. God gave you himself first by sending his Son. By his very nature, God is a giver: "For God so loved the world that he gave" (John 3:16). Your Father is generous.

One of our motivations for giving is, "I want to be like that. I want to emulate him in his generosity. I want to live up to the family name: to give, to bless, to sacrifice for the sake of others. Because that's how my dad is."

When you give, God sees. He sees you pouring out what you've been given, trying to be like him, and he says, "Oh, really? You think you can be as generous as I am? You think your arms are as big as mine? You think you can jump as high as I can? Well, watch this." And he pours it right back into your lap.

Bottom line, that is what giving is about—coming to see how good and powerful and loving and generous your Father really is. Not just having someone tell you about it, not just reading a verse about it, but experiencing it firsthand. In order to have that experience, however, you have to give him the opportunity. You have to open yourself up and give him something to work with.

So I dare you: get into a giving competition with your Father. If you do, I can tell you right now how it will turn out: you will lose, and he will win. And you'll both be happy about it.

16

He Might Make You Wait for It

In some cases, we don't have to wait very long to receive God's provision. There are times when he gives back to us almost immediately. I'll admit that I love it when it works that way—those times when it's quick and easy, without too much struggle.

But in my experience (and I don't have a verse from Scripture to back this up—it's just anecdotal), there's a bit of a beginner's-luck phenomenon here. The first few times you try faith-based giving, God tends to give the money back relatively quickly to let you know you're on the right track. As you mature, God may make you work a little harder for the blessing rather than fulfilling the promise immediately. He may even expect you to struggle with him in prayer, holding him to his word.

OUT OF ALL THE GIVING TESTIMONIES I've heard at our church through the years, the one that has moved me the most was from a woman who talked about how God *didn't* provide for her family, at least initially. I want you to hear it from her, the way it was recorded. Here is Amanda's story.

Last fall, when the Thanksgiving Offering rolled around, Ben [Amanda's husband] and I were less than enthusiastic. It had been a very tight year financially. And I mean, *really* tight. It wasn't a decision between the more expensive brunch place and the cheaper brunch place. It was a decision of should we go out to eat, at all, ever. We had been living paycheck to paycheck, and each month when rent was due, even that seemed to take some faith. So when it came time for the offering, our first reaction was tempered.

But we had always given to the offering in the past, and we wanted to be faithful, so we decided that we would give an amount that was equal to one month of tithe. It was a stretch, but it was theoretically doable.

But then, the week before the offering, something happened. I got strongly convicted that we were missing out on being a part of what God was doing by not taking bigger risks. Not that God needed us but that we had the chance to be more involved if we stepped out more. I knew that God would do amazing things, but I realized that if we weren't a part of it, we would miss out and wouldn't experience the joy.

So we decided to bet big. There was a particular job I had been hoping to get for some time—a dream job. Ben and I selected an amount to give based on what we would have been able to give if I got this job. It was seven times higher than the original number.

That was in November. Fast-forward to March. We had given some of what we had committed, but we were nowhere close to fulfilling our pledge. I was doing our taxes late one night, and no matter how many times I checked and double-checked my entries, the software kept saying that we owed a lot of money. It was money we simply didn't have.

I became so discouraged, so frustrated. It was time for God and me to have a little chat. I wish I could say it was a faith-filled, peaceful prayer in which I said, "God, I know you will provide. We trust you." But that's not what it was. Instead, I vented. And demanded. I remember having a conversation with God that went something like this:

> *Hey.*
>
> *You SAID . . . [At this point on the CD, Amanda's voice cracked; the next few paragraphs were said while choking back tears.]*
>
> *You SAID . . . that if we did this, you would be here.*
>
> *You SAID . . . that if we stepped out in faith, we would be part of something big.*
>
> *And I'm not seeing how this is adding up.*
>
> *What I see right now is that I didn't get the job, and instead of getting money, we now owe lots of money we don't have. I don't see how it's even imaginable to pay these taxes, much less our pledge.*
>
> *What's going on here, God?*
>
> *Just SHOW UP, would you?*

After praying that prayer, I went to sleep. The next morning, I woke up to find that I had clicked the wrong box somewhere, and it turns out the big tax bill was actually a large tax refund. So the immediate crisis was averted, but we still had nowhere enough money to fulfill our pledge.

Then, later that week—later that *exact same week*—I got an email. The email said that I had received a scholarship. It was a brand-new scholarship created that year for people who were graduating who fit exactly my profile.

The scholarship was exactly double the amount we had pledged.

It was absolutely a God thing that we would have missed out on if we hadn't taken such a big risk. It didn't work out the way we expected: I never got that job. But I got something better. I never could have imagined the blessing it would end up being for our family for me to work part-time for that season and be home with our kids, and the scholarship more than provided for our needs.

I CRIED THE FIRST TIME I HEARD Amanda tell her story live, and I've cried every time I've listened to the recording and every time I've read it while reviewing the drafts of this book. But there is one thing she said in her story that I disagree with. She said she wished she could have trusted that God had it all under control and prayed calmly and peacefully, implying that this is the way a more spiritually mature person would have prayed. Based on Scripture, I'm not so sure that's true. I believe the way she prayed is the highest type of prayer of all.

Far too often, our attitude toward prayer is that God knows best and God's going to do what God is going to do. We've been wrongly taught that "prayer doesn't change things; it changes us." (That's a lie from the devil.) We've been taught that prayer is the process of coming to God with our demands and then giving up on those demands, because we realize through prayer that they are selfish and unreasonable.

That picture of prayer could not possibly be further from the truth. It's not what we see in the Bible. The picture we get in the Bible is one of people making demands and holding God to them. Just as importantly, it's a picture of God absolutely loving this process.

How do you think God, as a Father, felt when Amanda prayed to him so earnestly through her tears—"But God, . . . you said." I'll tell you how I, as a father, feel about it. When my girls come to me, asking me to do something, and argue with me by saying, "But Dad, . . . you said," I love it. Why? *Because it means they take me at my word.* It means they believe that I'm a father who keeps his promises and that what I say can be depended on. What I say—my words— are a *fact* in their universe. Not a hypothetical but a solid certainty. In their minds, there's no gap between what I say and reality. If I say it, they count on it. "Dad said. So that's it. It's gonna happen." The few times that I have violated that trust—the few times that I have not made good on my word—I wanted to crawl under a rock and die. How could I do that to them?

I am an imperfect father. God is a *perfect* Father. The problem between God and us is never that he doesn't make good on his promises. The problem between God and us is that we don't expect him to. We refuse to come arguing and pleading like my girls do—like Amanda did: "But God, . . . you said!" We're too dignified for that.

That is the reason God will sometimes wait until the last minute to give. It's worth asking why God waited so long to provide for Amanda's family. Why did he hold back? The answer is simple: God waited because he hadn't gotten what *he* wanted yet. Through this giving contract, both parties are supposed to receive a benefit. Our benefit is greater faith and blessing and reward. But how does God benefit? He gets the one thing he most desires in all the earth: to hear our earnest prayers. He wants for us to talk to him with our whole hearts, not as a religious exercise, not with clichés, not out of duty, but as though we're talking to a real person. He was dying to hear Amanda cry out with her whole being, "But God, you said!"

And when he hears that, he starts beaming. His ears perk up, and he says with a smile and a wink, "Oh, did I? Oh, that's right, I did! I just wasn't sure you believed me. I wasn't sure you were listening. I didn't know if you really cared or if you felt like you needed me. But now that I see you do, let me show you how strong I am. Let me show you how good I am. Let me show you how ready I am to come to your aid."

One way of looking at this is that he's waiting for us to tell him who he is. He wants us to hold him to his own character. This might be the best way of making sense of the astounding conversation between God and Moses in Exodus 32:10–14 after the golden calf incident. God says to Moses:

> "Now leave me alone so that my anger may burn against them and that I may destroy them. Then I will make you into a great nation."
>
> But Moses sought the favor of the LORD his God. "LORD, . . . turn from your fierce anger; relent and do not bring

disaster on your people. Remember your servants Abraham, Isaac and Israel, to whom you swore by your own self: 'I will make your descendants as numerous as the stars in the sky and I will give your descendants all this land I promised them, and it will be their inheritance forever.'" Then the LORD relented and did not bring on his people the disaster he had threatened.

What was the gist of Moses's prayer? "But God, . . . you said." God was expecting Moses to hold him to his own promise. He's testing Moses: "Were you listening? Do you really believe I am who I say I am?"

It's the same with us when he withholds and delays in fulfilling his promise to give back to us and financially bless us in response to our giving. The more mature we become, the longer he'll expect us to wait and the more he'll expect us to claim the promise in prayer. Think back to the giving commitment Brittany and I made our first year of marriage. We saw him give back the first time within eighteen months and the second time a year after that, but the third part of the blessing didn't come for ten years.

He wants us to wrestle with him like Jacob did. He likes to wrestle with us. The intimacy of it fulfills him emotionally, just the way it fulfills me as a father to wrestle on the rug with my girls. God could have chosen to have a very civil, tame relationship with us, a relationship with no struggle, no roughhousing, but that's not what he wanted. You might remember that Israel, the new name that God gives Jacob, means "he who wrestles with God." What a tremendous name. I want that name; I want to earn that name as Jacob did. Do you remember what Jacob says as he's wrestling with God? "I will not let you go unless you bless me" (Gen. 32:26).

God expects the same tenacity from us. When you give expectantly, in response to God's promise to give back, your work isn't done. If the provision doesn't come at first, you have to keep believing until it does.

You must cling to God—grab hold of him and not let go—and say, "I held up my end of the deal, now you hold up yours. I will not let go until you bless me. Provide for me as you promised."

17

Too "Holy" for His Blessings?

n 2 Corinthians 8–9, Paul spends two entire chapters trying to motivate the church at Corinth to participate in an offering. What motives does he appeal to? Whatever they are, by definition these are the biblical motives for giving. Paul's way of motivating the Corinthians should be our model for motivating ourselves.

Let's begin with one of the more well-known arguments Paul makes, which is along the lines of, "You should give to others because Jesus has given so much to you." This is the essence of 2 Corinthians 8:9: "For you know the grace of our Lord Jesus Christ, that though he was rich, yet for your sake he became poor, so that you through his poverty might become rich."

There's no question it's a beautiful verse and a persuasive motivation. The trouble is that at many churches, 2 Corinthians 8:9 becomes the *only* acceptable motivation for giving.

I've heard some preachers and writers say that, as Christians, every good action we do should be motivated exclusively by gratitude. All should be done in response to what Jesus did for us on the cross. They call this "gospel-centered" motivation. If you believe that gospel-centered motivation is the only acceptable motivation—that the only good, God-honoring reason for taking an action is out of gratitude for the cross—then when you try to motivate yourself to give, you will just be saying some variation of 2 Corinthians 8:9 over and over again: "Give, because Jesus gave to me."

Likewise, if you believe that obedience is the best and highest motive, you will be saying continually, "Give, because God commands it." Or if you believe that altruism, compassion, and loving others are the highest motives, you will say, "Give, because of all the good it will accomplish in the lives of others."

To be clear, all of the above are excellent reasons to give, and all of them are mentioned by Paul in 2 Corinthians 8–9. But they aren't the *only* motives Paul mentions. He doesn't limit himself to gratitude, obedience, glorifying God, or wanting to help others. Rather, there is an *additional category* of motives, and these he actually emphasizes the most and lands on the hardest—motives that are completely self-centered.

For example, he appeals to the fear of negative consequences: "Give so that you're not embarrassed, and give so that I don't have to be harsh with you when I come." He appeals to a sense of pride and competition: "Give because

I've been bragging about what big givers you are, and give in competition with the other churches. Don't let them outgive you." But most important of all, Paul repeatedly tells the Corinthians to give out of a desire for personal gain: "Give because God will give back to you in proportion to whatever you give to him, give in order to receive."

Paul talks far more about these selfish motives than he does about being motivated out of gratitude for the cross, which receives only a single passing reference. Yet we've relied on the one verse because it sounds so noble and pure, and ignored all the other verses because they somehow feel less spiritual.

When confronted with 2 Corinthians 8–9, I finally had to ask myself, If Paul appeals to these selfish reasons to motivate his church, then why shouldn't I appeal to them to motivate my church? Do I think I'm nobler than Paul?

THERE IS A BIG REASON most pastors are afraid to talk about the selfish motives for giving: they are afraid of guilt by association. They don't want to be connected with the types of ministries that are famous for making these sorts of appeals.

Asking people to give with the expectation that God will bless them financially in response has long been a mainstay of hucksters and charlatans. Televangelists and "prosperity gospel" ministers have been teaching this principle for years. Many so-called ministers, through the effectiveness of this message, have raked in a sizable personal fortune they then spent on mansions and private planes.

It should go without saying that God will judge these men harshly. Nevertheless, many of us are guilty of sloppy thinking when it comes to how we respond to them. It's far too easy to say, "They fell into scandal; therefore, everything they said must be false." But it's not that simple. A more careful analysis would make a distinction between how they used the money once it was received and the message they preached to get that money in the first place. Just because the money wasn't put to good use doesn't necessarily mean that the message was wholly false.

I'd like to propose a radical hypothesis: What if the reason televangelists have had such success with these appeals to selfish giving is because it actually works the way they say it does? What if it's not a scam after all, and they've been telling the truth the entire time? What if the people who were giving to their ministries really were being blessed by God in response?

It's important to remember that when these people gave, they were giving to *God*, not to the minister. Just because the minister didn't use the money appropriately doesn't change the genuine faith that may have been active on the part of those who were doing the giving. God doesn't look at the *minister* when he decides whether to bless the *giver*. He looks only at the hearts of the givers themselves.

When we hear about financial scandals or embezzlement in churches, people often shake their heads and think, *What a shame. All the money those people sacrificed to give—it's all wasted, gone down the drain.* But my response to that is, "How do you figure? Do you think that what a pastor does with the money on earth is in any way going to affect the account balance of the givers themselves in heaven?"

WHAT I'VE FOUND is that many Christians, pastors and congregants alike, not only don't believe these rewards exist, they actually don't want them to.

I've heard people say things like, "You know, to be completely honest with you, this whole idea bothers me. The way you're talking about it just feels off. Do you really expect me to take this seriously? To listen to a pastor who says, 'If you give your money to the church, God will magically make money flow back to you'? At best, it seems way too good to be true. At worst, it seems like a scam of some sort. It feels so slimy, so crass—God providing checks in the mail and promotions and better apartments. Honestly, it's pretty embarrassing."

Bottom line, this objection comes from a place of snobbery. I should recognize snobbery when I see it: Manhattan is the snobbiest place on earth. This person is saying, "I'm too good for this. I don't need this." But by being sophisticated, by having more advanced tastes, by being above this sort of thing, they miss out.

I've noticed an interesting pattern. The more affluent and educated a congregation is, the more they dislike this idea of receiving financial provision from God. And the more they feel that it's beneath them. This makes sense: in general, snobbery increases in proportion to education and income.

On the other hand, I've found that poorer, less educated churches aren't as bothered by this principle. They talk about it often. Everyone knows this is how giving works, and they practice it and celebrate it. The reason poorer believers have an easier time accepting this principle is relatively obvious: they don't have much of a choice. They need God to provide for them. The more affluent, who have historically been able to provide for themselves, have the luxury of not depending on God if they so choose. If God makes them an offer, saying, "Give your money to me, and I'll provide for you in an exchange," the first thought of the self-sufficient is, *No thanks*. And so, because of their pride, the educated and sophisticated often miss out. As Paul puts it, "God chose the foolish things of the world to shame the wise" (1 Cor. 1:27).

Reward #4

Treasure in Heaven

18

It's Right to Expect a Payoff

In Mark 10:17–31, Jesus had consecutive conversations with two different men. These conversations are usually considered to be completely separate episodes. But if you read the chapter straight through, ignoring the headings in your Bible, it's clear that they aren't two episodes but one.

THE FIRST CONVERSATION, and the more famous of the two, is between Jesus and a "rich young ruler," or so this nameless man has come to be known. We mentioned this conversation in passing in chapter 5.

The man comes to Jesus with a question. He has become rich and influential at a young age. He has already climbed high on the ladder of success and is well positioned to climb higher still. This man reminds me of the men and women who make up our church. They work long hours and make good money. The text of the Gospel doesn't tell us how this man acquired his wealth, but it doesn't really matter. The point is that he was an ambitious high achiever who liked to win. He was accustomed to taking risks and making sacrifices in order to receive a bigger payoff. In other words, he knew how to play the game.

But the man was bothered by something. Though his place in this world had become secure, he had doubts about his status in the world to come. You almost get the sense that he'd been lying awake at night thinking, *OK, I'm set for this life . . . all the way through retirement. But what comes after that?* So he approaches Jesus and asks, "Good Teacher, . . . what must I do to inherit *eternal* life?" (v. 17, emphasis added).

Jesus's final words to the man seem like the ultimate call to selfless sacrifice. He tells him, "Go, sell everything you have and give to the poor. . . . Then come, follow me" (v. 21). If that was all Jesus had said, then it *would* have been the ultimate call to selfless sacrifice. He would have been telling this man to change his basic orientation toward life: "Stop seeking your own happiness and security. Stop being selfish. Think of others. Give all your hard-earned money to the poor; they need it more than you do. And then go become a monk for the rest of your life." But that wasn't all Jesus said.

If you read the passage too quickly, you may have missed something important, which *changes* the meaning dramatically. What Jesus actually says is this: "Go and sell all your possessions and give the money to the poor, and *you will have treasure in heaven.* Then come, follow me" (NLT, emphasis added).

This phrase "treasure in heaven" immediately raises all sorts of questions: What is it? How do we get it? Why is it better than treasure on earth? Will some people have more than others? Is it literal or metaphorical?

These questions deserve full responses, so we'll save them for a later chapter. For now, what matters is the following point: Jesus doesn't ask the man to give up all his possessions for nothing. He offers the man something in exchange. In that sense, he isn't asking the man to be unselfish at all. In a way, he almost *honors* the man's selfishness by addressing the exact concern the man approached him with. Because what the man was really asking was, "How can I be *as* happy and secure in the next life as I am in this one?" Jesus doesn't tell him to stop wanting that but simply says, "If that's what you really want, here's how to get it." The one sure thing is that whatever "treasure in heaven" means, it represents precisely the happiness and security the man was seeking. This is one of the few cases in which Jesus unambiguously answers the exact question the person asks.

When we see how the man responds, we get an inkling of why Jesus was rarely willing to answer questions so directly—we usually don't *want* to know the answers to the questions we ask. Answers back us into a corner. The rich young ruler has two (and only two) options with respect to Jesus's advice: he can take it, or he can leave it. The Gospels tell us that he chose the latter. The man simply turned around and "went away sad" (v. 22). He wasn't angry or offended. He didn't argue or ask any follow-up questions. He was simply *sad*. Jesus made him an offer, an offer that was in the man's own best self-interest, but he wasn't willing to take him up on it. Why not? We don't know. It could have been for any number of reasons.

Perhaps he didn't understand what treasure in heaven was, so it was hard for him to place a value on it.

Perhaps he lacked the patience to give up everything now for a reward so distant.

Perhaps he was afraid of what his life on earth would be like in the meantime, how much hardship he would have to endure before he received his reward.

Perhaps he just flat out didn't believe and thought Jesus was either lying or mistaken.

We have no idea which, if any, of those reasons are valid. All we know is that the rich man exits the scene, never to be heard from again.

BUT THE MOST IMPORTANT ASPECT of Jesus's conversation with the rich young ruler and what is often overlooked is that it's a setup for a second conversation that follows.

Peter, the most bullheaded of all of Jesus's disciples, had been eavesdropping. By the time the first conversation concluded, his wheels were spinning. Maybe he had never heard Jesus talk about heavenly treasure before. Or maybe he had simply failed to connect the dots and had not recognized how this concept might apply to him personally. But now, a thought occurs to him. True to his personality, he blurts it out, not thinking about how poorly it will come across: "We have left everything to follow you! What then will there be for us?" (Matt. 19:27).

In other words: "Jesus, I heard what you just said to that man. You told him that if he left everything to follow you, he would have treasure in heaven. My question is, Were you making that promise only to him, or is that something that applies to anyone? Because, just to remind you of the obvious, all of us have *already done* exactly what you suggested he do. We have already left everything we had to follow you. So when it comes to this treasure that you promised . . . um . . . I'm not quite sure how to say this, so I guess I'll just say it: What are we going to get?"

As onlookers to the scene, we cringe. The question is terribly awkward—a bald-faced, self-serving grab for personal riches. We marvel at how inappropriate Peter can be, how he continually sticks his foot in his mouth, and how he lacks the good sense to keep quiet. We compare him to the other disciples who very well may have been wondering the exact same thing, but at least they were smart enough to keep their mouths shut. But most of all, we wait; we wait for the stinging rebuke we know is coming. We are certain that Jesus will drop the hammer. We can almost hear his words before he speaks them. Something like:

"Peter, how could you be so selfish?"
"Peter, that's not for you to know."
"Peter, I am your reward. Am I not enough for you?"

To our astonishment, the rebuke never comes. Instead, Jesus's response to the question is even more shocking than the question itself, because Jesus answers Peter as though Peter had asked the most appropriate question in the world:

I assure you that when the world is made new and the Son of Man sits upon his glorious throne, you who have been my followers will also sit on twelve thrones, judging the twelve tribes of Israel. And everyone who has given up houses or brothers or sisters or father or mother or children or property, for my sake, will receive a hundred times as much in return and will inherit eternal life. But many who are the greatest now will be least important then, and those who seem least important now will be the greatest then. (vv. 28–30 NLT)

In other words: "Yes, that's right, Peter—of course it works the same for you. Do you think I'd make this offer to a man I just met but withhold it from my closest followers? The offer stands for the twelve of you as well. That man turned me down, but you've taken me up on it. And just as I promised him treasure in heaven if he were to forsake everything, so you will have treasure in heaven because you already have forsaken everything. When this world is all over and everything is made new and we start again, I'm going to sit on a throne, king over all. And right beside me will be the twelve of you, each in charge of your portion of my kingdom. Why? Because you've given everything. In fact, anyone who gives up comfort and prosperity for my sake will receive a reward in proportion to what they sacrificed, 100 times over, 10,000 percent interest. Which is the reason that many of those who have the least right now will very likely have the most then. Those who are at the bottom now will very likely be at the top then. Right now, that rich young man has far more than you do. But one day, the roles will be reversed. Peter, you are well on your way. You are going

170

to be rich. You are going to be famous. You are going to be powerful."

For those of us who have been raised with the view that it's always wrong to have selfish motives, this is the absolute last thing we expected Jesus to say. Not only are we taken aback, but we're also deeply confused. How could Jesus honor such greed? Doesn't he see how self-serving Peter is being? Why would he encourage this way of thinking? Doesn't Peter's question contradict everything Jesus stood for? Isn't it wrong to follow Jesus out of a desire for personal gain?

But the *real* Jesus isn't concerned with any of that. He doesn't mind the naked selfishness of Peter's question. It doesn't bother him in the least. In fact, the opposite is true: Jesus loved Peter's question, because it showed that Peter had taken Jesus's words at face value.

All through Scripture, there is one thing that exasperates God more than any other: when we refuse to take him at his word. He says things to us, and then we act as though he didn't say them. He tells us things, and then we act as though he must not be telling the truth. We ignore and disregard his plain statements.

How does it make Jesus feel to be treated like this? It should be easy enough to guess. How does it make us feel when people act as though our words aren't trustworthy? When someone assumes that we don't know what we're talking about?

This is what the rich young ruler did. He asked for Jesus's advice, then immediately decided not to follow it. And just at that moment, when Jesus was coming off the disappointing but all-too-familiar experience of being ignored, he is met with a breath of fresh air: Peter's simple, childlike, deeply human question: "Jesus, we did all that. What are we going to get?" The assumption behind the question is that if that is how Jesus says it works, then that must be how it works. And there is no other assumption that Jesus loves more.

Once again, we're confronted with a question woven throughout this book: What if we stopped worrying so much about whether we are being selfish—an issue that Jesus seems to care nothing about—and started worrying more about whether we are taking Jesus at his word?

19

Only a Fool Forgets about Death

he two conversations we looked at in the previous chapter aren't the only times when Jesus talked about the concept of *treasure in heaven*. In this chapter and the next, we're going to look at two more passages in which Jesus discussed this idea. Then in chapter 21, we'll consider what this treasure in heaven might look like.

IN LUKE 12:16–21, JESUS TELLS a story that has become known as the parable of the rich fool. It's short enough that I can quote it in full:

The ground of a certain rich man yielded an abundant harvest. He thought to himself, "What shall I do? I have no place to store my crops."

Then he said, "This is what I'll do. I will tear down my barns and build bigger ones, and there I will store my surplus grain. And I'll say to myself, 'You have plenty of grain laid up for many years. Take life easy; eat, drink and be merry.'"

But God said to him, "You fool! This very night your life will be demanded from you. Then who will get what you have prepared for yourself?"

This is how it will be with whoever stores up things for themselves but is not rich toward God.

Quick recap: the man is already rich. But then, he has an even more amazing year than usual, so amazing that he can retire early. On the eve of his retirement, just as he has finally earned enough to relax and enjoy life, he dies.

At first, it seems like quite a depressing story. Not only that, but the moral of the story feels a bit cliché, something we've heard plenty of times before. The idea that "you can't take it with you" has become an oft-repeated mantra. There's the line "You never see a hearse pulling a U-Haul," or the story about Rockefeller's accountant who, when asked how much Rockefeller had left behind when he died, replied, "He left all of it."

The inability to take wealth beyond the grave has been bemoaned by the wealthy since the beginning of time. (It doesn't bother those who are poor because, not having amassed any wealth, they aren't leaving much behind.) To the rich, death has always seemed terribly unfair. The idea of working so hard to build a fortune, only to surrender it, is maddening. It's what drove the pharaohs to bury their riches with them, in the hope that they could take them along or, if not, at least prevent anyone else from enjoying them. It's what drives today's wealthy to bequeath their fortunes to family members. "If I can't have it myself, at least it will stay in the family."

Ultimately, these solutions are all unsatisfying. One of the wealthiest men who ever lived was King David's son Solomon. He amassed what was probably the greatest private fortune of all time. But Solomon's peculiar curse was that he wasn't only the wealthiest man who ever lived, he was also the wisest. Which meant that he didn't have the luxury of blissful ignorance like the rich man in Jesus's story. The rich fool thought he had a great life—right up till the end. But Solomon couldn't shake the knowledge that someday his wealth would pass to another—which somehow seemed to take all the fun out of it. In the book of Ecclesiastes, he writes:

> Meaningless! Meaningless! . . .
> Utterly meaningless!
>   Everything is meaningless. (1:1)

> Whoever loves money never has enough; . . .
> As goods increase
>   so do those who consume them. (5:10–11)

> Everyone comes naked from their mother's womb,
>   and as everyone comes, so they depart. (5:15)

As I said a moment ago, we know all this. We know we're going to die; we know we can't keep our wealth. This has been observed for millennia by all the world's religions and philosophies. Is Jesus's parable of the rich fool simply another one of these depressing stories with the exact same point? Is it just a story about the meaninglessness of life and the futility of storing up wealth like something out of the book of Ecclesiastes?

The answer is no. To our great surprise, Jesus's real meaning is actually the exact *opposite* of that. And our clue is found in the word *fool*. That's what God calls the man: "You fool! This very night your life will be demanded from you. Then who will get what you have prepared for yourself?"

The more you think about it, the stranger the word *fool* starts to sound. It seems out of place, especially if you consider all the names God could have called the man instead.

On the one hand, God could have said, "You poor man." That would have been a statement on the man's misfortune. He would have been saying that the man was unlucky to die before he got to enjoy his wealth. No moral judgment, just pity.

On the other hand, God could have said, "You wicked man." By using the label *wicked*, he would have been saying that the man had done something morally wrong by keeping all his wealth for himself and not sharing it with those in need. He would have been judging the man for being too selfish.

But God doesn't call him either of those things. He doesn't comment on the man's misfortune, and neither does he comment on the man's moral character. Rather, what he comments on is the man's *intelligence*, or lack thereof.

It's not, "you wicked man" or "you evil man" or "you poor man" or you "selfish man." It's simply, "you fool." In other words, "You were dumb. You made a tactical error. You didn't think things through."

At first, this label seems ill-fitting, because we're talking about a savvy businessman. We expect that savvy businessmen may be immoral, but we don't expect them to be stupid. But that's what God calls this guy.

When God asks, "Who will get what you have prepared for yourself?" the implied answer is, "Not you. You won't get to keep it; it will pass to someone else." He is saying, "You didn't act in your own best self-interest. You did yourself a disservice."

But how so? The man couldn't have known he was going to die that night. And even if he had known, death is unavoidable. To call him a fool implies that he had some other, better course of action available to him. But what alternative is there? You cannot keep your money for yourself after death. That's what Solomon and all the wise men throughout the ages have said. So why does God call him a fool?

THE PHRASE JESUS USES that unlocks the mystery is "rich toward God." It's as if Jesus shakes his head and says, "It's a shame. This man was rich on earth when he could have been rich toward God instead."

This is a tantalizing possibility. It means that Jesus, unlike Solomon, sees a loophole. He sees a way to cheat death and taxes—those twin evils that are otherwise inevitable. And he's trying to let us in on it. Jesus says that instead of storing up his wealth in an account he was bound to lose, the man could have instead stored his wealth in an account he could keep. A bit later in the same chapter, he puts it like this: "Provide yourselves money bags which do not grow old, a treasure in the heavens that does not fail" (Luke 12:33 NKJV).

The rich man's treasure had *failed*. But Jesus says there is a treasure that doesn't fail. The rich man's moneybags went to someone else. Jesus says, "Provide yourselves money bags which do not grow old."

The rich man is a fool *not* because he surrendered his entire fortune but because he didn't have to. He could have kept it for himself—could have provided moneybags for himself—had he simply stored his treasure in heaven instead of on earth.

This raises the question of how exactly this storing of treasure in heaven is accomplished, and Jesus tells us that as well. Take a look at the sentence that comes just before "provide yourselves money bags": "Sell your possessions and give to the poor" (NIV).

The answer to the how question is remarkably simple. All that's necessary to transfer wealth from an earthly account to a heavenly account is to give it away. Whatever you hold on to, you lose. Whatever you give away, you keep. Or, as Jesus says in Luke 17:33: "Whoever tries to keep their life will lose it, and whoever loses their life will preserve it."

This statement doesn't refer only to martyrdom. It's a statement about *whatever* part of life we give up—as Jesus said to Peter, "Whoever gives up houses or family or property." Whatever we give up, we get to keep. Once you see that this is how giving works, you'll also see that it's simply the smart thing to do. Giving is not noble or altruistic. It's just prudent. Think back to the rich young ruler in the previous chapter. The reason he should have given his money away is not because that would have been the nice, loving thing to do, but rather because if he had done so, he could have kept it.

This is astounding: Jesus's argument for why we should give aggressively is based primarily on an appeal to our own self-interest. He does not say to give for the sake of the poor or even for God's sake. He says to give for our own sake. Like a wise financial planner, Jesus is simply dispensing advice about how to invest strategically: give away money you *can't* keep in order to earn money that you *can* keep." Or as Jim Elliot put it, "He is no fool who gives what he cannot keep to gain what he cannot lose."[1]

Did you catch the word Elliot used? "He is no *fool*." Unlike the man in Jesus's story, who was. The man's problem wasn't that he was selfish. His problem was that he was slow on the uptake—he was a fool.

20

If Others Reward You, God Won't

 have said in this book that many people feel it's wrong to give just because you're hoping God will bless you in response. They feel that if you give out of selfish motives—seeking some reward for yourself—then you haven't truly done a good deed. A verse that is often quoted in support of this position is Matthew 6:4: "But when you give to the needy, do not let your left hand know what your right hand is doing, so that your giving may be in secret."

A popular proverb paraphrases this verse: Blessed are they who receive without forgetting and give without remembering. The idea is that your giving should be so spontaneous, so selfless, that you don't even remember that you gave, and you certainly shouldn't be looking for some reward or recognition for giving. The term that's been coined to summarize this approach is *self-forgetfulness*. Many see it as a great virtue. But is that what Jesus is really talking about in this verse?

LET ME FIRST ACKNOWLEDGE the part everyone can agree on: there certainly *is* a wrong way to give, and Jesus is condemning it. In verses 2–4, he says:

> So when you give to the needy, do not announce it with trumpets, as the hypocrites do in the synagogues and on the streets, to be honored by others. Truly I tell you, they have received their reward in full. But when you give to the needy, do not let your left hand know what your right hand is doing, so that your giving may be in secret.

Jesus is calling out the Pharisees' approach as wrong. There's no question about that. The question is, *Why* is it wrong? What's so bad about it?

This is a critical question because, as it turns out, Jesus's reason for condemning the Pharisees' approach is not what we assume. We assume that trying to earn *any* reward for ourselves through giving is wrong, period; giving shouldn't be about gaining rewards at all. We've been taught that we should give out of a pure love for God and others or simply for the sake of giving itself. Now let's look at what Jesus says in the full passage:

> Be careful not to practice your righteousness in front of others to be seen by them. If you do, you will have no reward from your Father in heaven.

So when you give to the needy, . . . do not let your left hand know what your right hand is doing. . . . Then your Father, who sees what is done in secret, will reward you. (vv. 1–4)

Here's a question: If Jesus is telling us to give without thinking about the reward, then why does he promise a reward for our giving?

When Jesus says to give secretly rather than to be seen by others, the assumption is that our focus is to be on God and others, not on ourselves and what we might gain by it. But when we listen more closely, we find that this isn't what he's saying. He never says, "Don't think about yourself when you give" or "Don't give in order to be rewarded." Quite the opposite. Our desire to be rewarded is something he takes for granted. Beginning with that assumption, he then reasons with us, urging us to be careful when selecting the *source* of our reward. The source is to be our Father in heaven. There's nothing about forgetting self in this. Instead of telling us to stop thinking about our own interests, he encourages us to think about them more carefully.

WHEN JESUS SAYS that our Father will reward us for our giving, what sort of reward is he talking about? He tells us plainly, but we often miss his explanation because we think he's already switched topics. Immediately after discussing rewards in Matthew 6:1–18, Jesus turns to a discussion of treasures in verse 19. Most Bibles mark this transition with a new topical heading. But why would we assume that the rewards of verses 1–18 and the treasures of verses 19–21 are two separate things? Take a look at verses 18–21 as an integrated unit, without headings:

> And your Father, who sees what is done in secret, will reward you. Do not store up for yourselves treasures on earth. . . . But store up for yourselves treasures in heaven. . . . For where your treasure is, there your heart will be also.

Jesus's advice about choosing where to store our treasure is a continuation of his advice about choosing whom our reward will come from. He is repeating the same idea but in two different ways. First he says, "Don't seek a reward on earth from other people, when you could earn a reward from God instead." Then he says, "Don't store up treasure on earth, when you could store up treasure in heaven instead."

The common thread is that each of us has two accounts: earthly and heavenly. The point of giving—for that matter, the point of doing anything—is to make a deposit in one of these two accounts. The catch is, you must choose one or the other. The first verse in Matthew 6 says, "Be careful not to practice your righteousness in front of others to be seen by them. If you do, you will have no reward from your Father in heaven." He could likewise say, "Be careful not to store up your treasure on earth. If you do, you will have no treasure in heaven." It's either/or. We could also paraphrase Jesus's words like this:

> Of course you wish to be rewarded for your giving. Who would go to the trouble of giving if there were no reward? But don't be shortsighted—don't settle for a small reward now when you could have a greater reward later. Remember,

you'll only be rewarded once. If you give to receive praise from others, you sacrifice the reward from God. Far better to reverse that: give up the approval of your peers by acting in secret, in which case God will step in and offer a more lasting reward.

Just as with the rich young ruler and the rich fool, Jesus doesn't tell us that we're too selfish; he almost seems to be telling us that we're not selfish enough. Do you want a pat on the back now or treasure in heaven that will last for all eternity? Take your pick.

THIS PASSAGE CONVINCED me as a pastor that I should stay 100 percent ignorant of who gives what at our church. I have no idea who gives, and I have no idea how much they give.

There are several reasons for this. The first is that it makes it easier to treat everyone the same. James is very severe on churches where the wealthy get preferential treatment.[1] I've heard other pastors say they don't let a person's giving affect how they're treated. But in practice, this is very hard to carry out. It's almost impossible not to give more weight to the opinion of a big giver in your church than to someone who doesn't give at all.

The more important reason I like to remain ignorant of people's giving is because I don't want to preempt any of their heavenly reward by inadvertently rewarding them with praise now.

This underscores how different "giving" is from "fund-raising." I've never done any fund-raising at our church, and

I never will. In fund-raising, it's all about the praise now; recognition is the name of the game. When people give a certain amount, you print their name in the program or etch it on a plaque. If they make an especially large gift, you call them up and take them out to breakfast.

We could do that at our church, but the downside would be that all the big givers would be majorly gypped. Breakfast with me is a paltry reward. (Some people in our church might even think of it as a punishment!) And, as Jesus says, they'd be receiving that pathetic "reward" *in lieu of* a heavenly reward.

What's interesting about this either/or arrangement is that it provides a much stronger motivation for keeping your giving a secret than the standard moral norms of humility or modesty. This new perspective has the effect of making the thing you're not supposed to do—advertise your own giving—a lot less tempting.

Under the old, traditional interpretation of this passage—give for the sake of God and others alone—the admonition not to tell others about your giving is just a rule. It's a rule you know you should follow, but sometimes you are going to be tempted to break it. Because it feels good to receive praise, and if there's no penalty, why not enjoy the praise for a moment? You may start out intending to keep your giving a secret, but then it just slips out. "Whoops. Didn't mean to say that." Then you scold yourself: *I've got to be better about that. I messed up again. Jesus said not to do that. Stop seeking rewards for yourself! Stop doing these things to be noticed!*

Alternatively, what if it works the way Jesus says it works? What if every time you slip up and "accidentally" earn a reward for yourself from other people, you forfeit your reward and miss out on the treasure in heaven you would have received otherwise?

This completely changes the strength of your motivation. Now you want to keep your giving a secret, not because you're doing the right thing but rather out of self-interest. If you slip up, it's not, "Tsk tsk," but rather, "You fool!" You just traded the reward of God for a pat on the back. All that sacrifice, and nothing to show for it.

21

Rewards Are Still a Gift of Grace

et's begin this chapter by summing up every-thing we've learned about treasure in heaven thus far. Fortunately, all the passages we've looked at point in the same direction. Based on these passages, we can draw two conclusions.

First, the main advantage of treasure in heaven is that you get to keep it, as opposed to treasure on earth that you're bound to lose one way or another. In Matthew 6:20, Jesus refers to moths that destroy and thieves who steal. In Luke 12:33, he refers to purses that wear out, letting money drop out the bottom. Today, instead of moths, thieves, and worn-out purses, we talk about a fluctuating economy, stock market crashes, fraud, depreciation, and so on. Regardless of the specifics, the point is the same: wealth on earth is fragile. Even if you do manage to keep it safe during your lifetime, you'll surrender it when you die. That's the point of the parable of the rich fool. This is how it goes with treasure on earth. Treasure in heaven, on the other hand, doesn't carry any of these risks. It's guaranteed.

Second, sending your treasure from earth to heaven is a very simple process. All that's required is that you give the money away while on earth. In Luke 12:33, Jesus told the crowd: "Sell your possessions and give to the poor. Provide purses for yourselves that will not wear out, a treasure in heaven that will never fail." Which is exactly what he told the rich young ruler: "Sell everything you have and give to the poor, and you will have treasure in heaven" (Mark 10:21). It's also what he said to Peter: Whoever gives up houses, family, or property "will receive a hundred times as much" (Matt. 19:29). Jesus repeats the same thing to different people.

Putting all that together, we can summarize everything we know about treasure in heaven in three points:

1. There are two types of wealth—earthly and eternal.
2. Eternal wealth is better than earthly wealth because it's permanent.
3. You can convert earthly wealth to eternal wealth by giving it away while you're still living.

Paul himself provides a similar summary in a letter to Timothy: "As for the rich in this present age, charge them not to be haughty, nor to set their hopes on the uncertainty of riches, but . . . to be generous and ready to share, thus storing up treasure for themselves as a good foundation for the future" (1 Tim. 6:17–19 ESV).

Paul's mention of the "uncertainty of riches" parallels Jesus's teaching about moths, worn-out purses, and death.

His reference to a "good foundation" parallels Jesus's statement that heavenly wealth "will not fail." And, like Jesus,
he points to the possibility of converting earthly riches to
heavenly treasure by being "generous and ready to share."

Scripture, then, is entirely consistent. That's what we
know so far. But it still leaves open an all-important question: What exactly *is* this treasure in heaven?

OUR TROUBLE BEGINS with the word *treasure* itself.
Though it's undoubtedly the most literal, technically correct translation of the Greek word *thesauros*, which appears
in these passages, it is nevertheless a terrible choice.

Here's why. What matters in translation isn't just literal
correspondence but also subconscious association. In the
English language as it is spoken today, we no longer use the
word *treasure* unless we're talking about pirates. And I don't
mean modern-day Somali pirates but the eighteenth-century
swashbuckling type from stories and movies. It's impossible
for a native English speaker to hear Jesus talk about treasure
in heaven without being whisked away to Treasure Island or
Neverland. It feels like fantasy.

But what Jesus is talking about has nothing to do with
wooden chests or an X marking the spot. To figure out what
he's actually referring to, let's go back to the Greek word
thesauros. You probably recognize it; it's where we get our
English word *thesaurus*. That's because *thesauros* is not only
the Greek word for "treasure" but also the Greek word for
treasury. *Thesaurus* is short for *thesaurus verborum*, a "treasury of words."

Instead of thinking of treasure itself, we'd be much better off thinking about "treasu*ries*" and "treasu*rers*." What do treasuries hold, and what do treasurers deal with? Not "treasure," but money. And money, plain and simple, is what Jesus is talking about in these passages.

You've got to banish the word *treasure* from your mind. Many other words are better: wealth, riches, prosperity, affluence, material abundance. But *money* is probably the best word of all. To get closest to what Jesus meant, we should understand it like this: Do not store up money on earth, but store up money in heaven.

I'll admit, the idea of there being money in heaven is something that feels wrong to almost everyone, at least initially. But we have a choice to make. We can either plug our ears and choose to believe that heaven is the way we wish it were, or we can listen to what Scripture says. And heaven, according to Scripture, is a real place, every bit as real as the room you're in right now. Not only is it a real place, but also it's filled with real stuff: real trees, real streets, real buildings—and real money.

That's not to say that wealth in the next life will be exactly the same as wealth in this life. Of course not—everything will be different in heaven. It's not that heavenly wealth and earthly wealth are identical; it's just that they're similar, the same type of precious objects. The reason we know this is because Jesus always talks about them together.

WHAT IS IT EXACTLY THAT BOTHERS us so much about there being money in heaven? I've found that people primarily have three problems with the idea.

The first problem is that many people feel something like this: "Even if I believed there was money in heaven, it would be hard for me to care about it. Why will I need it? If heaven is perfect, will I even notice whether I have more or less money? I don't get it."

Personally, I can relate to that feeling. I don't know how money in heaven will work or why we will need it. I do know that we shouldn't allow our inability to comprehend the idea of money to undermine it. The thought behind this idea is very straightforward: just as there are richer and poorer in this life, there will be richer and poorer in the life to come. That sentence strikes most people as controversial, but it is obvious based on New Testament teaching. And just as richer is preferable to poorer in this life, so it will be in the next. If you like wealth now, you're going to like wealth then. Just because you're not able to pin down the exact nature of that wealth shouldn't keep you from recognizing that wealth is better than not-wealth. When you get there, it will be concrete enough— whatever it is—that you're going to be happy you have it.

The second problem goes like this: because some will have more and some will have less, it's hard for us to imagine that we won't feel envy or disappointment. If others have more treasure in heaven than we do, won't that make us sad or jealous?

But this question comes from seeing heaven through earthly eyes and assumes we'll still have our sin natures. In this life, if someone has more than we do, we often feel dissatisfaction. It won't be that way when sin is removed. Jonathan Edwards put it best:

> It will be no damp to the happiness of those who have lower degrees of happiness and glory, that there are others

advanced in glory above them. . . . Those who are not so high in glory as others, will not envy those that are higher, but they will have so great, and strong, and pure love to them, that they will rejoice in their superior happiness . . . so that instead of having a damp to their own happiness, it will add to it. They will see it to be fit that they that have been most eminent in works of righteousness should be most highly exalted in glory. . . . Then will be fulfilled in its perfection that which is declared in 1 Corinthians 12:26, "If one of the members be honored all the members rejoice with it."[1]

Again, I'll admit this is difficult to wrap our minds around. But Paul said, "For now we see through a glass darkly" (1 Cor. 13:12). Rather than worry about how God will sort it all out, we ought to act based on what he has clearly told us. And the one thing there is no question about is that heavenly treasure is something he wants us to *seek* because it motivates us to give away our money now. If you let yourself get tied up in knots with questions about how you're going to feel in heaven—so that you're no longer motivated to seek heavenly treasure now—you've missed the point. A wise Christian would simply reason, "I will leave that to God and do what he expects me to do: build up as much treasure in heaven as I can by giving away as much as possible, and then some."

The third problem is perhaps the most serious: it bothers people that treasure in heaven is something we can *earn*. The objection goes like this: "I thought I was saved by grace and not by works. I thought I got to enjoy the glories of heaven not because of anything I did but only because of what Jesus did. How does the idea of rewards based on giving square with the idea of grace?"

It's a great question. In response, I'll say two things.

First, in the final analysis, it's still all grace. It's all grace that God would *let us* operate under this arrangement at all. He didn't have to offer us rewards for our giving; he could have just demanded that we give without offering any incentive. And it's only by his gracious power working within us that we can ever do any good thing, including giving, to begin with. So everything Paul says in Romans about boasting being "excluded"[2] still fully applies. Any good thing we do comes from God.

In 1 Chronicles 29, David leads the people of God in an offering for building God's temple. The people rise to the occasion, giving above and beyond what was expected. Afterward, David gives thanks to God: "But who am I, and who are my people, that we should be able to give as generously as this? Everything comes from you, and we have given you only what comes from your hand" (v. 14).

That's exactly right. Who are we? Who are we that we should receive the honor and privilege of giving? God gave the money to us just so we could have the joy of giving it back to him. Even our giving is a gift from him.

Every Christmas I open gifts from my daughters. These are gifts they bought with their "own money." But where did that money come from? From me. I gave them their allowances. In other words, they couldn't give anything to me unless I *first gave to them*. It's all my money. It started with me, and it ends up back with me in the form of a gift. But in the process, they get to experience the joy of giving, and I get to experience the joy of seeing them give.

So too with God and us. It's all his money. We couldn't give anything to him unless he first gave to us. So it's still all grace.

Here's another way to think about it. If life is a board game, and we get rewarded for doing certain things (such as giving) within the game, that doesn't change the fact that God made the game. He laid out the board, he gave us the pieces, he set up the prizes. So who are we, anyway? "What is mankind that you are mindful of them?" the psalmist asks (Ps. 8:4). The fact that we will be rewarded based on our actions in no way nullifies or decreases the magnitude of God's grace. If anything, it gives us an even greater appreciation for it.

The second thing that I will say about grace is that it's only through the death of Christ—and God's gracious forgiveness of our sins—that we could ever stand before him to be judged by our good works, giving or otherwise. In this respect, Christianity differs markedly from every other religion.

In other religions, the basic concept of judgment by works is that of a moral scale. On one side of the scale is the good you've done, and on the other side is the bad. At the end of your life, if the good outweighs the bad, you'll be rewarded. If the bad outweighs the good, you'll be condemned. Thus, in other religions, giving your money away (or any other good deed) can be a way to balance out your sins.

That is not what the Bible teaches. The Bible says that for every one of us, the bad will always outweigh the good, no matter how much we give away or how much good we do. That's because God looks at the heart, and even our best acts, including our most sacrificial gifts, are stained with sinfulness. Left on our own—without God's grace and for-giveness—we don't have a chance. As the psalmist puts it, "If you, LORD, kept a record of sins, . . . who could stand?" (Ps. 130:3).

Does the death of Christ do away with the moral scale altogether? Not exactly. It's often presented that way, as if Jesus's blood wipes the entire "works" ledger clean. But if that were true, it wouldn't matter what we do. Good or bad, everyone would be equal.

Instead, what happens is that the bad side of the ledger gets erased—our sins are blotted out—and the good side stays. If you are in Christ, no one will remember the mis-takes you made, but everyone *will* remember and celebrate the good you did, and you'll be rewarded for it. The sins are forgotten, but everything you did for God and gave to God is still to your credit. That's grace.

22

The Ultimate Reward
Is Friendship

The parable of the shrewd manager in Luke 16:1–8 is the last parable on the theme of heavenly treasure. This final passage might be the most helpful of all in terms of connecting us on an emotional level with the concept of treasure, because in this story Jesus puts a different spin on things. He tells his disciples the following story:

> There was a rich man whose manager was accused of wasting his possessions. So he called him in and [said], . . . "You cannot be manager any longer."
>
> The manager said to himself, "What shall I do now? My master is taking away my job. I'm not strong enough to dig, and I'm ashamed to beg—I know what I'll do so that, when I lose my job here, people will welcome me into their houses."

So he called in each one of his master's debtors. He asked the first, "How much do you owe my master?"

"Nine hundred gallons of olive oil," he replied.

The manager told him, "Take your bill, sit down quickly, and make it four hundred and fifty."

Then he asked the second, "And how much do you owe?"

"A thousand bushels of wheat," he replied.

He told him, "Take your bill and make it eight hundred."

The master commended the dishonest manager because he had acted shrewdly. For the people of this world are more shrewd in dealing with their own kind than are the people of the light. I tell you, use worldly wealth to gain friends for yourselves, so that when it is gone, you will be welcomed into eternal dwellings.

Jesus holds this man up as an example because the man does something smart once he finds out that he's going to lose his job, that his time is up. Being fired is a metaphor for death. All the money the man has been managing is going to the owner, and he won't be able to earn a commission on it any longer. One of the points of the story is that the same is true for each of us. We are all stewards, managers, of the money that has been entrusted to us. One day we'll have to give that money back to the owner.

So what does the shrewd manager do? He calls all those who owe money to his boss and says, "I'm about to get fired, so I don't care what my boss thinks anymore. Which means I can do you a favor; let me cut your debt in half." He's not doing this to hurt his boss; he's doing it to help himself. He's afraid he won't be able to find another job after he is let go. But he thinks, "If I do a bunch of favors, I'll make some new friends. Then, when I have no income, I'll at least have a place to stay."

And Jesus says, in so many words, "You've got to hand it to the guy; it's a smart move." Why? Because he's using something he's about to lose anyway—control of his employer's accounts—to secure for himself benefits that will last even after he's been fired. It costs him nothing, but he gains a great deal.

When people first read this story, they get hung up on the guy's dishonesty. They wonder how he can be commended as a good example if he's dishonest. But Jesus isn't commending his dishonesty. Rather, he's intentionally using a dishonest character to underscore the point we've seen in several other passages—that is, what you do with your money isn't primarily an issue of virtue or morality but one of intelligence and preparedness.

This man sees what's coming, and he prepares accordingly. He knows what's going to end—his relationship with his boss. And he knows what's not going to end—his relationship with the people he helps. So he sacrifices the one for the sake of the other. He gives up something he is unable to keep in exchange for something that will last—the friendships.

Compare this behavior to that of the rich fool in Jesus's other parable, who wasn't dishonest but foolish. He did not make preparations. He just kept hoarding as if life were going to go on forever. When the end came, he had nothing to show for himself. Jesus is telling us to be like the shrewd manager, who thought ahead, and not like the rich fool, who lived in denial.

THE MAIN VALUE of the parable of the shrewd manager for us is that it presents a different way of thinking about eternal riches. Jesus changes up the imagery somewhat. The idea is the same: trade your money on earth for riches in heaven. But this time, Jesus doesn't talk about treasure in heaven in terms of cold, hard cash. Rather, our treasure is friendships. He says to use our wealth now to make friendships that will last forever so that our friends will welcome us into their homes. What does this mean?

It means at least two things. First, it means that the people we help with our wealth now—people who are needier than we are in this life—are probably going to be wealthier than us in the life to come. Remember, everything is upside down in the kingdom of God. The first shall be last, and the last shall be first. There's nothing we can do about that. But if we use our money to care for *them* now, they'll enjoy caring for *us* later with their resources. This truth is emphasized in the story of the rich man and Lazarus.[1] If the rich man had helped Lazarus when they were both alive, Lazarus almost certainly would have helped the rich man after death.

But the idea of making lasting friendships has a second and more important meaning. We're not to use our money to help only those who are materially needy but also those who are spiritually needy, people who haven't yet heard the gospel. Jesus doesn't only commission us to care for the poor. He also commissions us to take his message to the ends of the earth. *Both* of these commissions require a lot of money to carry out. But it's in the context of the second and greater of these commissions that the idea of new friends welcoming us into eternity takes on a whole new meaning. We are now talking about people who are *there* in the kingdom of God because of us. If we give our money to help reach people who haven't heard the good news, then when these people are in heaven because of our sacrifice, we'll have friends who welcome us into their homes. We'll have our reward.

In 1990, the blockbuster Christian song of the year was "Thank You" by Ray Boltz. The gist of it is that when this guy goes to heaven, people he has never met come up to him and say, "Thank you." He doesn't know why, so they have to explain themselves. One says, "I was in your Sunday school class, and you were the first person who told me that God loves me, and that's why I'm here." Another one says, "You gave money to that missionary, and that missionary told me about Jesus, and that's why I'm here." And as they keep coming, he looks and sees this long line of people, as far as the eye can see, waiting to thank him. The man begins weeping as they come, one by one. Jesus says, "Child, look around you; great is your reward."

That's a great picture of what Jesus is talking about in the parable of the shrewd manager. When you give your money away in this life, you're sacrificing only something that will eventually be worthless for something that will last forever—people. When you get to the other side, when you get to heaven, you will see what money is able to accomplish. I can guarantee that you are going to wish you had given more.

That is also the point of the final scene of *Schindler's List.* You remember the story. Schindler is a war profiteer and a member of the Nazi party. But as he sees what's happening to the Jews who are employees in his factory, he starts bribing Nazi officials to keep certain Jews out of the concentration camps, essentially buying them more time to live. When the war finally ends, all the people he gave bribes for get to go on living because of him. The entire three-hour film builds to this one final scene in which everyone he saved gathers to thank him. As he's looking at their faces, he is not filled with joy but rather with the deepest possible remorse. He realizes that as much as he did, he could have done more. He starts looking around at his possessions. He looks at his car and says, "This stupid car. Why didn't I sell that? Why didn't I use it for bribe money? This could have bought me ten people. This pin, this swastika pin, it's made of solid gold. This is two people, two lives, two souls, for this ridiculous pin. What was I thinking?"

And he is overcome; he falls to his knees, sobbing.

THE REASON THE SCENE IS SO POWERFUL is because it's not just Schindler's situation. It's not just a situation faced by some Germans during World War II. It's exactly the same situation we all find ourselves in, the same situation Jesus is talking about in the parable. There is an astonishing opportunity available to every one of us to trade money for people, to give money and get eternal friendships in return. And Jesus tells us not to miss this opportunity, because when it's gone, it's gone. You will lose the money one way or another. The question is, Will you have anything to show for it when your time is up?

Conclusion

Why Give to a Church?

et's say you agree with the idea of giving in general, and you agree that you should be giving aggressively—an increasing percentage of your money each year. Even so, why should you give to a church in particular rather than to some specific cause you're passionate about? In fact, many scriptural passages talk about giving to the poor. Does giving to a church count as giving to the poor? I'll address these questions in this conclusion.

Following are the top three reasons why a significant portion of your giving should be through your local church.

REASON #1: When you give your money to your church, you are giving to the poor because your church helps the poor.

Or at least I assume it does. If your church doesn't help the poor, you should find another church. Scripture is clear that one of the church's functions is not only to preach the gospel but also to physically help and defend those who are vulnerable.

Depending on the size of your church, it will often be easier (and more efficient) for your church to give money to organizations that help the poor and fight injustice rather than set up ministries within the church to do this same work. This is the decision we made at our church. We could have started our own homeless shelter, but why not financially support the Christian homeless shelter down the street instead? We could have started a ministry to fight sex trafficking or to offer legal services to those who can't afford it, but it didn't make sense to do so given the fact that there are already great Christian ministries that do these.

Instead, we made it a goal at our church to give away a higher percent of our budget each year to organizations that help the poor and disadvantaged. We are therefore modeling, on an institutional level, what we're asking the people in our church to do on an individual level. It would be odd, to say the least, if we encouraged the people in our church, "Give more. Trust God. Don't build bigger barns to stockpile wealth," and then we as a church built bigger barns to stockpile wealth.

I firmly believe that the reason our church has never had a financial shortfall is because we give so much away. We trust that if we direct funds to these outside organizations involved in work that God cares about, he will provide enough to meet the church's budgetary needs. It works the same for individual families as it does for the church as a whole.

At our church, we are now up to giving away 33 percent of our total intake each year to other organizations. For every three dollars we receive, one dollar goes right back out the door. I believe that God has so increased the giving at our church that 66 percent of this God-blessed amount is actually more than 100 percent of what we'd be getting if we weren't giving anything away. And I look forward to seeing the percentage we're giving away climb to 40 percent in the years ahead.

But back to the main point of reason #1. If your church helps the poor, then when you give to the church, you are giving to the poor. And what's critical is that you are helping the poor in Jesus's name. As Jesus says in Mark 9:41, "Truly I tell you, anyone who gives you a cup of water in my name . . . will certainly not lose their reward."

What does it mean to do something in Jesus's name? It means doing something in such a way that Jesus gets the credit. When you give to the poor through your church (rather than directly to the organizations that help the poor), this is exactly what happens—God gets the credit. Our church has developed a reputation in our city for caring about the city's needs. By pooling our resources and giving it collectively as a congregation, it makes Christ look good.

REASON #2: When you give your money to your church, you are giving to God himself in a more direct way than when you give to other organizations.

An interesting passage on this theme is John 12:3–7, where Mary of Bethany gives Jesus an expensive gift:

Then Mary took a twelve-ounce jar of expensive perfume . . . and she anointed Jesus' feet with it. . . .

But Judas Iscariot, the disciple who would soon betray him, said, "That perfume was worth a year's wages. It should have been sold and the money given to the poor." . . .

Jesus replied, "Leave her alone. . . . You will always have the poor among you, but you will not always have me." (NLT)

Given all the clear scriptural testimony about giving to the poor, the point of the passage is obviously not that we shouldn't give our money to the poor. Rather, the point of the passage is that Jesus himself is more precious than any cause or need that may present itself. There is a certain sense in which gifts given to Jesus will always be "wasteful." He doesn't need them, and they could be given to someone who does. And yet, Jesus accepts this expensive gift as an appropriate expression of gratitude, devotion, and worship.

The church is Christ's body. This is more than a metaphor; it is a metaphysical truth. The church is actually the body of Christ on earth, his presence here until he returns. Therefore, gifts given to the church should be thought of as being given to Christ himself.

Similarly, in the Old Testament when God ordered the building of the tabernacle and then later the temple, he asked the political and religious leaders to lead the people in an offering. They gave extravagant gifts for these two building projects, far above what was asked, which enabled ornately beautiful structures to be erected. But they weren't giving because they believed in a cause per se. There were better, more useful ways the money could have been spent. Rather, they were giving to God himself as an expression of gratitude and as a statement of trust in his provision for them. The wastefulness of the opulent buildings was part of the point.

The bottom line is that Christian giving is not about giving to a cause; it's about giving to a person. In this, it differs from every other type of giving. When you give to the church, you are giving a gift of thanks to God who breathed life into you, the same God who poured out everything—even life itself—to welcome you home with open arms even after you turned your back on him.

There is a certain excessive generosity and impracticality to the whole thing, somewhat like the generosity and impracticality of spending a significant amount of money on a diamond for an engagement ring. Could the money for that diamond be spent on far more important causes? Of course, but it's a statement of love.

When you're trying to determine the best or most important cause to give to, you employ a calculating, utilitarian form of reasoning. Gifts given to God should come from a totally different place.

REASON #3: When you give your money to your church, you are giving to the most important and worthwhile "cause" on earth.

Notwithstanding everything in reasons #1 and #2 about why we shouldn't give to a cause, it's nevertheless the case that there is no cause greater than God's church.

There is no cause that has done more good for the human race as a whole, in tangible, earthly terms, than God's church.

Much misinformation exists on this point. Detractors will sometimes get away with making the absurd claim that the church has done more harm than good. This is a ludicrous, laughable assertion.[1]

And if you take an eternal perspective and look at the church's work of reconnecting people to God, then nothing even comes close in importance. Someday the world will be remade, and God himself will right all wrongs. All poverty and injustice will end. The only work that must be completed before that happens is the proclamation of the gospel: that Christ died and rose again for us and that new life in him is possible. As we said in chapter 22, the church's mission isn't to help only the poor but also the poor in spirit. And no other organization can do that work.

If you are a Christian, the question for you is, What cause could you possibly care more about than the church? What cause could possibly be more important than building the kingdom of God and advancing God's work in the world? This is the prayer of Jesus: may "your kingdom come, your will be done, on earth as it is in heaven" (Matt. 6:10). This is why Christ came, and this is why his body, the church, still exists on earth. When we financially support the church, we participate in God's work.

Notes

Introduction

1. Ruth Moon, "Are American Evangelicals Stingy?," *Christianity Today*, January 31, 2011, https://www.christianitytoday.com/ct/2011/february/areevangelicalsstingy.html; Meera Jagannathan, "How Much Money Should You Be Giving to Charity?," MarketWatch, September 24, 2018, https://www.marketwatch.com/story/how-much-money-should-you-be-giving-to-charity-2018-09-24.

Chapter 1 Decision

1. Matt. 6:1–4.
2. Rom. 9:1–3.

Chapter 3 Deliverance

1. "Poverty Makes Financial Decisions Harder. Behavioral Economics Can Help," January 20, 2016, PBS, https://www.pbs.org/newshour/economy/poverty-makes-financial-decisions-harder-behavioral-economics-can-help.

Chapter 4 Declaration

1. Exod. 3:1–15.

Chapter 6 Your Money Represents Your Life

1. James 2:18.

Chapter 8 There Is No Faith without Action

1. "Is Luther Really the Originator of 'We Are Saved by Faith Alone, but the Faith That Saves Is Never Alone'?," Christianity Stack Exchange, edited, September 21, 2015, https://christianity.stackexchange.com/ques tions/42366/is-luther-really-the-originator-of-we-are-saved-by-faith -alone-but-the-faith-t.

Chapter 9 Giving Is the Perfect Test of Faith

1. 1 Cor. 15.

Chapter 11 Materialism Is a Religion

1. 1 Kings 18:21.

Chapter 12 Giving Is the Only Way Out

1. Max Weber, *The Protestant Ethic and the "Spirit" of Capitalism* (Australia: Allen and Unwin, 1930), 181.
2. Edmund Burke, *The Works and Correspondence of the Right Honourable Edmund Burke*, vol. 5 (London: Rivington, 1852), 259.

Chapter 15 Why It Works This Way

1. Matt. 6:32, emphasis added.
2. Sam McBratney, *Guess How Much I Love You* (Somerville, MA: Candlewick Press, 2008).

Chapter 19 Only a Fool Forgets about Death

1. Elisabeth Elliot, *Through Gates of Splendor*, rev. and updated ed. (Carol Stream, IL: Tyndale, 1981), 3.

Chapter 20 If Others Reward You, God Won't

1. James 2:9.

Chapter 21 Rewards Are Still a Gift of Grace

1. *Works of Jonathan Edwards*, vol. 2, sermon 8, Christian Classics Ethereal Library, May 29, 2019, http://www.ccel.org/e/edwards/works 2.xv.viii.html.
2. Rom. 3:27.

Chapter 22 The Ultimate Reward Is Friendship

1. Luke 16:19–31.

Conclusion

1. For more on this, check out any of the books by Rodney Stark from the past twenty years, especially *The Victory of Reason*.

Ryan Thomas Holladay (writing as Ryan Thomas) grew up in California and was educated at Wheaton College (BA Philosophy), Union Theological Seminary (MA Theology), and NYU School of Law (JD). He then served as the lead pastor of Lower Manhattan Community Church in New York City for ten years. Currently, Ryan lives in Kigali, Rwanda, with his wife and four daughters.

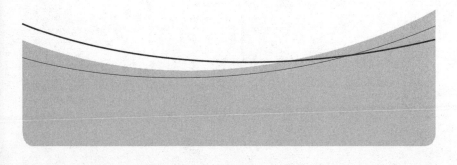